The First Americans

by
Juan Schobinger

William B. Eerdmans Publishing Company
Grand Rapids, Michigan

Originally published as *Le origini. I primi Americani*
Copyright © 1994 Editoriale Jaca Book spa, Milan
All rights reserved

English translation copyright © 1994 by
Wm. B. Eerdmans Publishing Co.
255 Jefferson Ave. S.E., Grand Rapids, Michigan 49503

Editorial and graphic design: Editoriale Jaca Book, Milan
Cartography: Studio Andrea Dué, Florence
Editing and layout: Antonio Maffeis
Large color plates:
parts I, II, III Antonio Molino
part IV Claudia Vanagolli
part V, VI Giorgio Bacchin

Color separation by Graphicservice, Milan

Printed and bound in Italy

00 99 98 97 96 95 94   7 6 5 4 3 2 1

Library of Congress Cataloging-in-Publication Data
Schobinger, Juan.
    [Origini. English]
    The first Americans / by Juan Schobinger.
    p.   cm.
    ISBN 0-8028-3766-2 (cloth)
    1. Indians — Antiquities. 2. America — Antiquities.
I. Title.
E61.S36 1994
970.01—dc20   94-22543
                                                              CIP

Contents

PART I

The Ancient Inhabitants of the Americas	5
Geography and Natural Regions	8
Natural History: Pleistocene and Holocene	12
The History of Scientific Research	16
The First Inhabitants: Hunters and Gatherers of the Protolithic	20
The First Inhabitants: The Hunters of the High Paleolithic	24
The First Inhabitants: The Hunters and Gatherers of the Andes	28
Petroglyphic Art (Rock Painting and Sculpture)	32

PART II

The American Neolithic	37
The Earliest Farmers and Ceramists	40
The Argentine Northwest	44
The Ancient and Middle Village Period	48
The Late Village Period	52
The Southwestern United States	56
The Ancient Hohokam, Mogollon, and Anasazi	60
Anasazi-Pueblo	64

PART III

The First Metropolis: Teotihuacán	69
Geography and Natural Regions	72
The History of the Research	76
Prehistoric Forerunners: Preceramic Agriculture	80
The Preclassical	84
The Culture of Teotihuacán: The History	88
The Culture of Teotihuacán: The Art	92
The Culture of Teotihuacán: Politics and Religion	96

PART IV

The Olmecs and the Maya	101
Geography and Natural Regions	104
Olmec Culture: The History of the Discoveries	108
Olmec Culture: The Art	112
Mayan Civilization: The History of the Discoveries	116
Mayan Civilization: The History	120
Mayan Civilization: The Art	124
Mayan Civilization: The Religion and Writing	128

PART V

The First Andean Empire: Chavín	133
Geography and Natural Regions	136
The History of the Research	140
Preceramic Villages and Temples	144
The Temples of the Valley of Casma	148
The Culture of Chavín: The Lanzon	152
The Culture of Chavín: The Art	156
The Chavín Horizon	160

PART VI

The People from the Center of the World: Tiahuanaco	165
The Classic Period: Nazca and Mochica	168
The Forerunners of Tiahuanaco	172
The Earliest Phases of Tiahuanaco	176
The Great Periods of Tiahuanaco	180
The Great Monuments of Tiahuanaco	184
The Great Periods of Tiahuanaco: The Imperial Stage	188
The Late Period	192

Painting in red of two horned figures carrying weighted atlatl and spears.
Sierra di Kilo, Chihuahua, Mexico.
Redrawn by Green (1966).

PART I

The
Ancient Inhabitants
of the Americas

A view of the Grand Canyon from the South Rim. The Colorado River runs along the floor.

The Uspallata Valley and the Tunduqueral Ridge, Mendoza Province, Argentina.

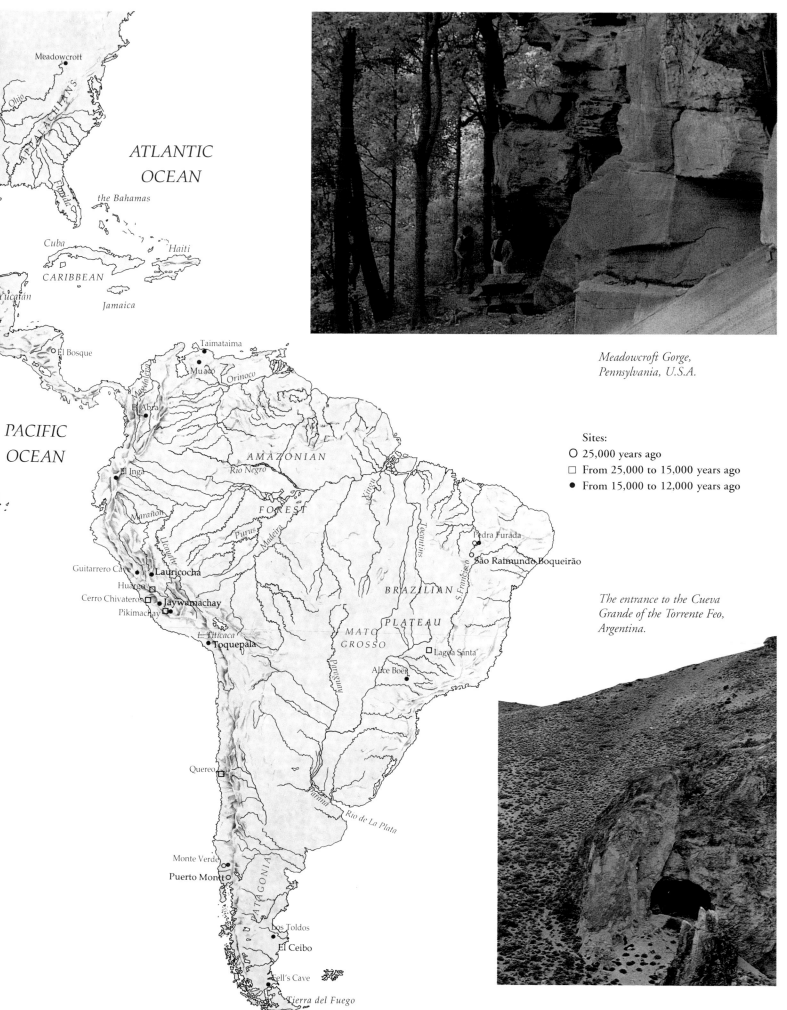

ATLANTIC
OCEAN

the Bahamas

Cuba
Haiti

CARIBBEAN

Jamaica

Yucatán

PACIFIC
OCEAN

Meadowcroft

Ohio

Florida

El Bosque

Taimataima

Muaco

Orinoco

El Abra

AMAZONIAN

Rio Negro

FOREST

El Inga

Marañon

Purus

Madeira

Ucayali

Guitarrero Cave

Lauricocha

Huargo

Cerro Chivateros

Jaywamachay

Pikimachay

L. Titicaca

Toquepala

Xingu

Tocantins

BRAZILIAN

S. Francisco

Pedra Furada

São Raimundo Boqueirão

PLATEAU

MATO
GROSSO

Lagoa Santa

Alice Boer

Paraguay

Quereo

Paraná

Rio de La Plata

Monte Verde

Puerto Montt

PATAGONIA

Los Toldos

El Ceibo

Fell's Cave

Tierra del Fuego

Meadowcroft Gorge,
Pennsylvania, U.S.A.

Sites:
○ 25,000 years ago
□ From 25,000 to 15,000 years ago
● From 15,000 to 12,000 years ago

The entrance to the Cueva
Grande of the Torrente Feo,
Argentina.

1 Geography and Natural Regions

BEFORE WE BEGIN to describe a major historical process, we must set it in a physical context. Since the geographical details of the American continent can be found in any atlas or reference work, let it suffice to say that what we commonly refer to as the western hemisphere is actually made up of two continental masses that just happen to be joined by the isthmus of Panama (a strip of land that lay underwater until the end of the Tertiary period. These landmasses are known as North and South America. In turn, the northwestern extremity of North America is just barely separated from Asia by the Bering Strait, while the far northern aspect of the continent — the coasts and island formations of modern Canada — is bounded by the icy Arctic Sea. The tundra that covers this broad expanse of territory stretches unbroken to the west, across Siberia. This land is inhabited by Eskimos, an aboriginal people that came from northern Asia. To the south there is a vast region, covering nearly all of Canada, the most distinctive feature of which is extensive conifer forest. The western portion of this region is mountainous, and the Pacific coastline and the numerous associated islands have a rainy climate. The great territory that extends further southward — what is now known as the United States — has a temperate climate. Environmentally, this area is marked by a greater variety: huge deciduous forests to the east, plains and steppes in

the central region west of the Mississippi River, and further west the Rocky Mountains, which run the length of North America and feature a vegetation not unlike that of the European Alps. Between the Rockies and the western coast can be found extremely varied landscapes, including prairies, valleys, and mountains (in particular, the massif of the Sierra Nevada), all of which are characterized by a relatively arid climate.

South of the Tropic of Cancer we find the so-called "Central-American funnel." The northern section of this region is semiarid, while the central area features a highland ranging in altitude from 2,000 to 2,500 meters (6,600 to 8,200 ft.), girded by a chain of tall volcanoes, and swept by seasonal rainfall. Along the coasts of the Gulf of Mexico and the Pacific Ocean are tropical rainforests, far more rich in vegetation than the higher regions. The rest of Central America and the archipelago of the Antilles support a more markedly tropical vegetation.

On the other side of the funnel lies South America, shaped something like a huge triangle, the northernmost tip of which (the Goajira peninsula, in Colombia) lies at about 12 degrees North latitude. The easternmost tip (Cabo Blanco, in Brazil) lies just south of the equator. The third tip of the triangle (Tierra del Fuego and the adjacent islands) lies past 55 degrees South. The total land area of the continent is just over 17,800,000 square kilometers

The McBride Glacier in Glacier Bay National Park, Alaska (aerial photograph).

(6,880,000 sq. mi.), and the bulk of it lies near the equator, roughly between 10 degrees North and 30 degrees South. In this respect, the continent has more in common with Africa than it does with North America: much of the continent enjoys an oceanic type of climate, with cool summers, mild winters, and relatively limited variations in temperature.

The Cordillera of the Andes is another fundamental feature of South America, forming a sort of continental spinal cord. The Andes extend from Venezuela and Colombia in the north all the way south to the furthest islands of Patagonia, with peaks that tower nearly 7,000 meters (24,000 ft.). Mount Aconcagua in western Argentina is the highest point in the Americas.

The entire chain of the Andes, from north to south, is covered with vegetation, varying in type, extension, and altitude according to the distance from the equator. Temperatures in the Andes generally correspond to the latitude: torrid from the Car-ribean coasts down to about 20 degrees South latitude; temperate and humid from that latitude all the way down to the area around the Strait of Magellan; and very cold in the far south. Precipitation is quite abundant in the northern, central, and eastern sections of the continent (with the exception of the semiarid territory of the caatingas, in northeastern Brazil). In the Andes and the sub-Andean regions, the climate is semiarid, and almost no rain at all falls in the strip of land along the Pacific coast from northern Peru to northern Chile and in the desert of Atacama. Each of these climatic zones supports characteristic vegetation: there is dense equatorial jungle along the Amazon River and its tributaries, bordered by immense areas of savannah; desert flora in the caatingas in northeastern Brazil; forests and cerrados (savannah) further south; prairies and steppes in the flatlands of Uruguay and Argentina; and typical sub-Antarctic vegetation in Chile and southern Argentina.

Fajada Butte stands at the southern entrance to Chaco Canyon in New Mexico (U.S.A.), wrapped in morning mist.

Two different environments suitable for human settlement in arid or semi-arid regions. Above, *a river oasis in the desert region of Nazca, Peru.*

(Photograph by Orefici)

Left: *The bottom of Frijoles Canyon in New Mexico (U.S.A.), featuring the important archaeological site of Tynyi.*

2 Natural History: Pleistocene and Holocene

JUST AS in other places on earth, great climatic changes took place in North America during the Pleistocene (1,800,000 to 10,000 B.C.E.), the geological age that immediately preceded our own. A great continental sheet of ice almost entirely covered what is now Canada. This continental ice sheet, now known as the Laurentian Glacier, extended from Hudson Bay in the north along the Atlantic coast south and inland far beyond the St. Lawrence River and the Great Lakes region. (The Great Lakes are, in fact, residue of the final thaw.) The glacier covered much of what is now the United States. In four known cycles of glaciation, which geologists now refer to as the Nebraska, Kansas, Illinois, and Wisconsin stages, ice reached south as far as the areas now occupied by these states. The western reaches of the Laurentian Glacier formed a broad arc that at its greatest extension reached all the way over to the glaciers that today still flow down from the Rocky Mountains in southern Alaska and British Columbia. On the other hand, the broad valley of what is now the Yukon River was then free of glaciers.

During the periods in which the continental glacier advanced, a phenomenon known as *eustacy* occurred — there was a worldwide drop in sea level proportional to the amount of ice contained in the glaciers. It is easy to grasp the workings of this phenomenon if we consider that precipitation is for the most part the result of evaporation from the

ocean bodies. During a period of great glaciation, the precipitation remains in the form of snow and ice on dry land and hence cannot replenish the volume of the ocean.

Following the eustatic drop in the level of the Bering Sea, which is a relatively shallow body of water in the first place, a "land bridge" was formed — a strip of land that emerged from the ebbing waves. This bridge, known as Beringia, played a fundamental role in the history of the population of the American continent. Paleontologists have uncovered evidence of the migration of more than forty animal species from Siberia to North America, including mammoth, reindeer, caribou, bison, musk ox, and elk. There is evidence of fewer than ten species migrating in the opposite direction, from North America to Asia. Among the most important of these species were ancestors of the camel, wolf, horse, and — in a later period — foxes and American woodchucks. It is believed that hunters in the Paleolithic Age who lived in northern Siberia crossed the land bridge into North America to keep up with their migrating prey.

It seems most likely that human migration into North America would have been possible only under two conditions: the existence of a permanent land bridge between Siberia and North America and the formation of an ice-free corridor between the two vast glaciers that then existed in what is now Canada. A number of scholars believe that both these conditions were met during three specific periods:

1. from 50,000 to 40,000 years ago
2. from about 28,000 to 25,000 years ago
3. from 13,000 to 10,000 years ago.

These and many other of the dates that will be cited in subsequent pages were determined through carbon-14 dating.

The phenomenon of eustacy recurred with each glacial period. There were rises in the sea level (known as *transgressions*) during the interglacial periods, and drops (known as *regressions*) during the glacial periods. Sea level dropped and rose by as much as 150 meters (nearly 500 ft.). The regression during the Wisconsin stage was substantial enough to uncover the Beringian land bridge and allow animals and humans to migrate from one continent to another.

The Pleistocene is considered to have been definitively over once the great glacial ice sheets retreated to the area that they now occupy. This process occurred slowly, and by fits and starts, between 15,000 and 8000 B.C.E.

Over the course of the last two or three millennia of this process, a number of the larger Pleistocene species became extinct. Among them were the mammoth, various types of protocamelids, the horse, various sorts of bison, and the giant ar-

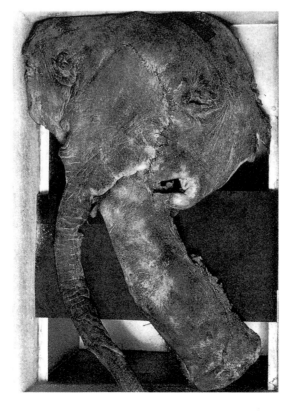

Beringia was at first used as a land bridge only by animals. This photograph shows the carcass of a young mammoth discovered in Alaska.

madillo, which had migrated from southern America. Just why these extinctions occurred is unknown. In all likelihood, there were a number of causes, undoubtedly linked to the sharp climatic shifts of the period.

We have a good deal less knowledge about the events of the Pleistocene in South America. Among the things that we do know, however, is that there was no land bridge linking the two American continents at the beginning of this period. The Isthmus of Panama was submerged.

Concerning the human population of the continent, we can safely say that it did not originate in South America. In all likelihood, humans arrived in small groups of hunter-gatherers, after crossing the Central American isthmus during a period a regression, in much the same way that their forebears had reached North America by crossing the Beringia land bridge. We have no reliable evidence that this happened before the last period of great glaciation, the Wisconsin stage.

South America was affected by glaciation to a far lesser degree than was North America. Ice formations were consolidated only in the far south, covering what is now known as Tierra del Fuego and the area of the Patagonian Andes as far north as the thirty-ninth parallel South. A great many lakes in this are remain as evidence of the ancient glacial formations.

The glaciers began to retreat across the various affected landmasses around 15,000 B.C.E. After periods of considerable oscillation, the climate began to stabilize in the cycle that is now familiar to us. The current epoch forms part of the geological period we call the Holocene, which began about ten thousand years ago. Paleogeographic studies indicate that, with few exceptions, glaciers had retreated to their current locations and territories by about 9000 B.C.E.

In the first few millennia of the postglacial period, higher temperatures and levels of humidity encouraged the growth of forests throughout the territory that had been occupied by glaciers. In North America, this period is known as the Hypsithermal. It ended around 4000 B.C.E. and was succeeded by a period of cooling and increased aridity (at least in the Andean region). Toward the end of the Pleistocene and during a number of different phases during the Holocene, there were episodes of intense volcanic activity. In South America, for a

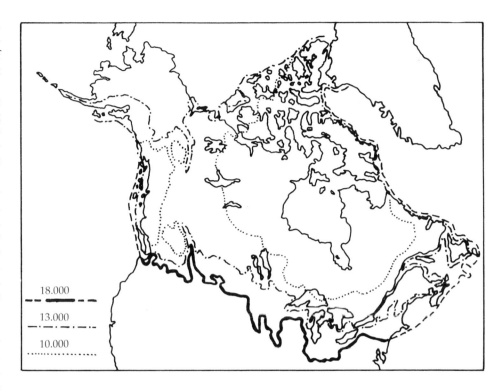

Approximate chronology (Estimated according to diverse methods)	America	Europe
1,000,000 years ago	Nebraska	Günz
700,000 years ago	Kansas	Mindel
300,000 years ago	Illinois	Riss
70,000 years ago	Wisconsin	Würm
10,000 years ago	Postglacial	Postglacial

18.000

13.000

10.000

number of reasons, more than one genus and species of the fauna that typified the Ice Age became extinct. The rise in sea level associated with the retreat of the glaciers took place very slowly, and it was not until 4000 B.C.E. that sea level approached something like its current level.

The tropical regions of the northern hemisphere oscillated between periods of drought and relatively temperate periods during the Holocene. The Amazonian jungle grew back slowly, gradually expanding by taking over strips of savannah and semiarid caatinga surrounding it. It appears to have reached its current size as late as about 2000 B.C.E. In contrast, the zones that we now refer to as the Cuenca della Plata and northern Patagonia appear to be substantially the same as they were during the Pleistocene.

Phases of deglaciation in North America.

Comparative chart showing the names of glacial periods in Europe and in America.

Pages 14-15, top: *Roden Crater, Arizona.*
(Photograph by James Turrel, from the archives of the Panza di Biumo Collection)

Pages 14-15, bottom: *the course of the central Rio Marañon, immersed in the impenetrable Amazonian forests.*
(Photograph by Mireille Vautier)

3 The History of Scientific Research

THE ORIGIN of the Amerinds (a name used by anthropologists to refer to the aboriginal population of the American continents, in place of the term "Indios" mistakenly used by Christopher Columbus) was the subject of great speculation from the era of the first explorers onward. It was not until the twentieth century, however, that theories began to be developed on a scientifically sound basis. We will consider three of these theories here, giving the names of the scientists who developed them and noting in parentheses the dates in which they were first presented.

Florentino Ameghino (1900-1910), an Argentine paleontologist, theorized — on the basis of an

evolutionary approach and a number of discoveries of bones and rock fragments — that the aboriginal population of the Americas originated in the Pampas and Patagonia, and then spread throughout Asia and other parts of the planet during the course of the Tertiary period.

Ales Hrdlicka (1910-1935), a North American anthropologist and physicist, differed with Ameghino over the existence of a "fossil" American human, which he ruled out completely. Hrdlicka maintained that the American continents were populated by humans from Asia following the retreat of the glaciers of the Pleistocene; he believed that the Asian settlers were ethnic Mongolians who arrived sometime after 8000 B.C.E. and immediately took up agriculture. He believed that the Americas had never been home to Paleolithic human beings. He allowed that archaic humans might have settled the continent, working upon their previous experience in Asia.

Paul Rivet (1924-1943), a French ethnologist, made comparative studies of the cultures of Oceania and those of the Americas, observing a number of parallels that he later explained with a theory of multiple origins. Rivet held that humans first arrived in the Americas from Siberia, just as Hrdlicka claimed, but that other groups later arrived in the Americas from the Pacific: Australoids (from Australia and Tasmania), Melanesians, and Polynesians. Rivet also included Eskimos in his list of the more recent immigrants. Among the followers of Rivet are José Imbelloni and Salvador Canals Frau.

Prior to the development of carbon-14 dating in 1950, archaeologists had recourse to only a very limited body of written documentation, and it was insufficient to provide an adequate framework for researchers. Many of those publishing at that time had been trained in other areas of specialization and were inclined to rely on methodologies involving nothing more than a hypothetical "reverse projection" of ethnographic, linguistic, physical, and anthropological data. The progress made since then in terms of methodology and field research has allowed us to formulate new and substantially more compelling theories.

Regarding the matter of the earliest settlement of the American continents, scholars now universally agree that, contrary to Hrdlicka's belief, there were Paleolithic humans in the Americas. Archaeologists have gathered convincing evidence of a human presence in the Americas during the late Pleistocene.

We still don't know — and probably never will know — exactly when the first human set foot on the soil of the New World after crossing the land bridge of ancient Beringia. In theory, this initial immigration could very well have taken place prior

Greatest extent of Beringia (about 20,000 years ago). The most important sites in which bone and stone remains have been found are shown.

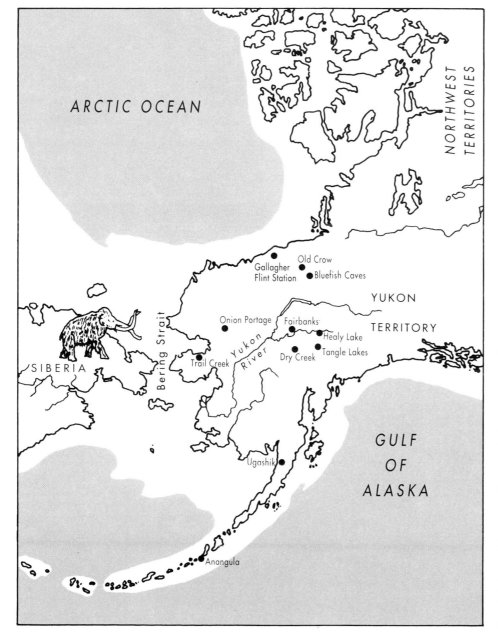

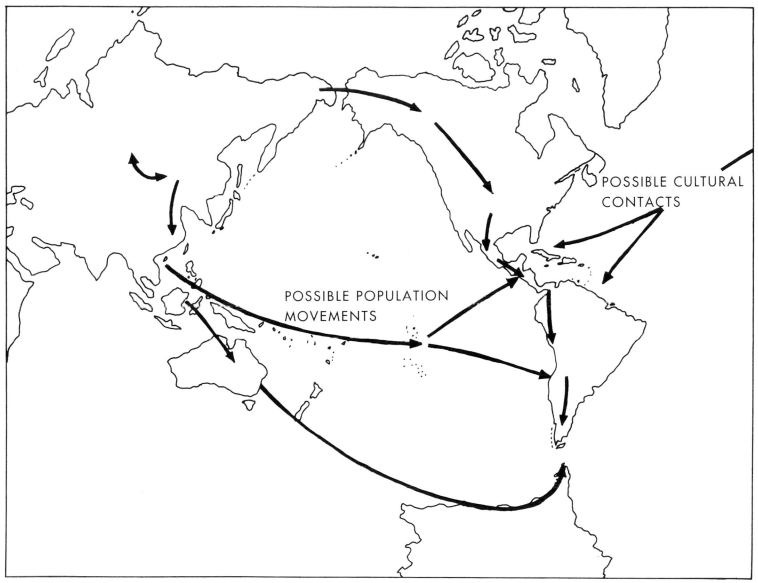

The routes indicated in the theories of how the Americas were populated.

to the Wisconsin stage of the Ice Age, during the Illinois stage, by which time continental land bridges had already formed and humans had fully mastered the arts of making and controlling fire, which would have been a fundamental resource for crossing the frozen wastes. It has, in any case, been solidly established that the earliest human settlements in the Americas date at least as far back as the first or second phase of the Wisconsin stage (i.e., some 70,000 to 60,000 or some 50,000 to 40,000 years prior to the Christian era, respectively).

Some archaeological evidence has been adduced in support of Rivet's theory of trans-Pacific migration, although there is no definitive proof. If migrations from the Pacific regions did occur, however, they could not have taken place prior to the third millennium B.C.E.

This map shows the western half of
North America and the eastern tip
of Asia. The lighter blue indicates the
territory covered by glaciers during
the glaciations, while the darker blue
shows the different areas of land
that emerged following the roughly
100-meter (330-ft.) drops in sea level.
Over this land bridge, the earliest
groups of Homo sapiens were able
to migrate from Asia to Alaska, later
descending, through a passageway
that opened up amid the ice, toward
the center of the North American
continent.

4 The First Inhabitants: Hunters and Gatherers of the Protolithic

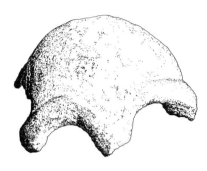

Human skullcap from one of the caverns of Lagõa Santa (Minas Gerais, Brazil).
(Drawing by J. Ferrari, based on work by A. Bryan)

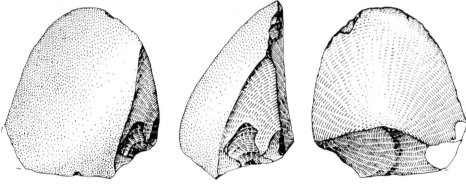

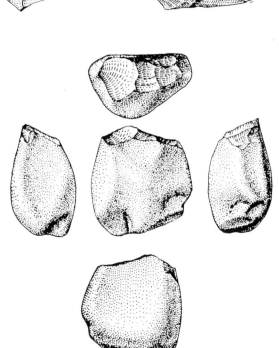

Ancient stone implements from Toca da Esperança (west of Bahia, Brazil). This flake struck from quartzite stone, with signs of work along the edge, is more than 40,000 years old.
(Based on work by H. de Lumey et al.)

From the same site and of the same age: a hatchet (worked stone) made of quartzite. The lìthic industry was similar to that in the zone of São Raimundo Nonato.
(Based on work by H. de Lumey et al.)

THE CRADLE of humanity is unquestionably located somewhere in the huge triangle formed by the continents of Europe, Asia, and Africa. It is in the latter of the three continents that the most ancient paleoanthropological remains and artifacts have been found. In Australia and America, the earliest traces of humanity date from the Pleistocene. We do not know the reasons why certain groups moved northeast from the Pacific coasts of what is now China and Siberia. It may be that these early migrants were simply following animal migrations, taking advantage of the relatively mild climatic phase that occurred during the Wisconsin glacial stage, crossing Beringia, and moving on into the Yukon River valley. In any case, many groups made the trip, not just one, and probably many of these early migrants made return trips to Asia. Those who remained in present-day Alaska and northwestern Canada may have guessed that there were lands further south and waited for the best time to set out for them.

That time came with the formation of what is referred to as the "ice-free corridor" that developed during the interstadials of the Wisconsin stage of glaciation. This corridor, varying in width, cut diagonally across the present-day Canadian provinces of Alberta and Saskatchewan. It was sealed off for the last time when the two great ice sheets joined at the height of the Wisconsin stage, which corresponded roughly with the European Würm III period (20,000 to 15,000 B.C.E.).

The ancient settlers who fished and gathered along the seashores had another available route south to the American continent. The Pacific coastlines offered an open passage from the Aleutian Islands to the coast of what is now Vancouver, where the glaciers of British Columbia ended, and further south to the temperate valleys and forests of what is now the northwestern United States and then to the sunny lands of present-day California, which were then far less arid than they are today.

As it turns out, evidence of the American Protolithic has been found in four locations in southern California and a fifth in the high Yukon valley, in the extreme northwest of Canada. In this last location, the Old Crow site, artifacts have been found that were probably made from bones of animals that have long since become extinct, dating from 40,000 to 25,000 B.C.E. In the same region, the Bluefish Cave site has yielded rock and bone fragments dated from 25,000 to 12,000 B.C.E. that seem to establish the existence of a considerable tradition of primitive technology associated with the settlers' adaptation to a harsh climate. As of this writing, we know of no protolithic sites in any areas closer to the likely entryway to the American continents.

The locations in California where the most ancient protolithic sites were found are:

1. The Calico Mountains in the desert some 200 kilometers (125 mi.) east of the present-day city of Los Angeles. Here, the remains of roughly cut flakes of stone have been found that date back to the beginning of the Wisconsin stage (80,000 to 50,000 years ago).

2. China Lake, two hundred kilometers (125 mi.) north of the Calico Mountains, on the southern slopes of the Sierra Nevada. This prehistoric lake, now quite dry, contained the remains of a lithic industry, with large flakes associated with mammoth bones dating back 42,000 years.

3. Mission Valley, which is today on the eastern outskirts of the city of San Diego. Along the enormous terracings that surround the town, remains have been found of a lithic industry dating back about 100,000 years. (This age estimate is still under discussion; if it is confirmed, then Mission

Valley would certainly push back the date of the first settlement of the Americas.)

4. Islands off the coast of southern California that were once solidly attached to the continent. Mammoths lived in this territory when the land was peninsular; when the peninsulas became islands, the isolated mammoth population underwent gradual genetic changes that produced a dwarf mammoth population. Later, paleo-Indian hunters reached the islands. On the island of Santa Rosa (at the archaeological site of Wooley Mammoth), human remains have been found that date back from 40,000 to 25,000 years.

Stone and bone artifacts have been found at sites in Central and South America as well, including the following: El Cedral (30,000 B.C.E.) and Tlapacoya (22,000 B.C.E.) in Mexico, Puerto Montt in southern Chile (31,000 B.C.E.), and São Raimundo Nonato in Brazil (40,000 B.C.E.). In the northeastern regions of Brazil, the remains of rock paintings have been found, dating from 10,000 to 5000 B.C.E., according to Nièvde Guidon.

We have no information about the physical structure of the earliest Americans. In all likelihood they were variants on the early "Neanderthaloid" man (or "presapiens"), whose remains, dating from the high Pleistocene, were found in China. Other humans, the descendants of groups that entered the Americas after 30,000 B.C.E., were quite similar to the modern, or "Australoid," race. And Australoid man may have lived in the northern territories of Asia prior to the expansion of the "Mongoloid"

race, thus providing a further confirmation of Rivet's theory.

During the late glacial period — after the peak of the Wisconsin stage — the glaciers began to retreat, and it is from this period that we can date what archaeologists call the "transition sites," until the period of the "higher hunters." In particular, we should take note of the caves of Meadowcroft, near Pittsburgh in the eastern United States, which is considered the most ancient site of the period. These caves were occupied by a group of humans who possessed a lithic technology that differs sharply from that of the Protolithic. Their principal remaining artifacts are made of fragments of flint, but they also include a stone point 4.5 centimeters (1.75 in.) in length, with engraving on both sides.

The intermittent presence of these groups can be dated back to between 14,000 and 9300 B.C.E.; the flint arrowhead dates from 10,800 B.C.E. Does this indicate a new migration from Asia? This is not clear. The fact that the route from the northern regions may not have been entirely passable during this period would seem to argue in favor of a local development, which clearly occurred in parts of South America. The Peruvian cave of Pikimachay has been dated to this transition period. Other examples include the Patagonian caves of Los Toldos and El Ceibo (10,600 B.C.E.), and the site of Monteverde in southern Chile (11,000 B.C.E.), where an entire protovillage has been unearthed in a virtually intact state, providing a priceless record of prehistoric settlement on American soil.

Reconstruction of the community of Monte Verde. The village had both residential and nonresidential areas. This illustration looks north across the stream of the Chinchihuapi. The residential areas were arranged along the eastern section of the north bank and along the south bank. Most of the furniture, wooden utensils, and mortars were found inside the homes. The nonresidential area, where the igloo-like building was found, occupied the western portion of the village on the north bank. Most of the mastodon bones and complex stone tools — worked and cut on both faces — were deposited in an irregular circle around this building. They were found together with plants that probably had medical applications.

(Based on work by Dillehay)

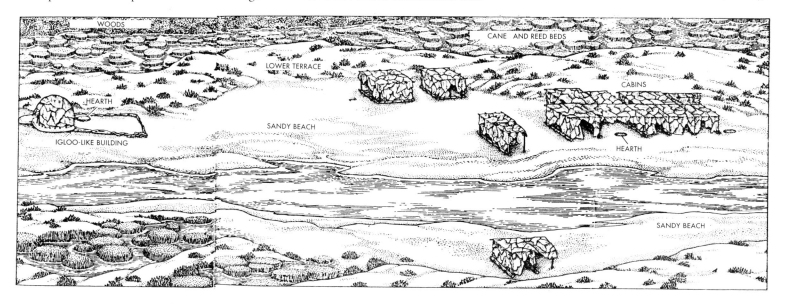

WOODS
CANE AND REED BEDS
LOWER TERRACE
HEARTH
SANDY BEACH
CABINS
IGLOO-LIKE BUILDING
HEARTH
SANDY BEACH

Facing page: *Rock paintings by the Archaic Gatherer Peoples, with depictions of plants linked to anthropomorphic figures.*
(Photograph by Anati)

The gorge at Meadowcroft, Pennsylvania, where the earliest stone tools from the late Ice Age (dated between 14,000 and 11,000 B.C.E.) were found.
(Photograph by the author)

5 The First Inhabitants: Hunters of the High Paleolithic

Below, right: *A diagram of the princi-pal groups of higher hunters of the late Pleistocene epoch in North America and the Caribbean basin area. The two broken lines to the north indicate the approximate boundaries of the great glacial areas in the regression phase of circa 8,500* B.C.E.
A: the region of the "ancient culture of the cordigliera" (from 9,000 B.C.E.).
B: the nucleus of the zone of "the great plains culture (Llanos)" (from 10,000 B.C.E.*) and probable migration routes. Three transitional sites dating from between 12,500 and 11,000* B.C.E.:
(1) *Meadowcroft;* (2) *Wilson Butte Cave;* (3) *Fort Rock.*

THE SECOND major cultural development in the history of the Americas was that of the the hunters of the High Paleolithic. This transition was marked by a more complex and specialized industry than that developed by the hunters and gatherers of the Protolithic, and was comparable to that of the High Paleolithic in the Old World. A number of scholars add the term "paleo-Indian" to the term Paleolithic, but it is probably advisable to remain with the uni-versally recognized terminology of American High Paleolithic. The most important common feature of the period is that of the presence of well-made stone points.

By 10,000 B.C.E. the glaciers that had long covered all of present-day Canada and the far northwest of the United States were in full retreat. The glacier that was centered on Hudson Bay formed a vast semicircle, the edge of which arched to the north of the Great Lakes and east of the Mackenzie River, while the glacier that covered the Rocky Mountains survived only at the highest alti-tudes, along the Pacific coast.

In the meanwhile, the ice-free corridor had widened considerably, facilitating communications with Beringia. At this point, in a number of differ-ent areas of the present-day United States, the first High Paleolithic hunters began to settle almost im-mediately, either absorbing the late Protolithic groups or replacing them entirely. The arrival of the new hunters may have resulted from new migra-tions from the North or through local development of transitional groups, but it is most likely that the changes took place through both of these processes.

We have learned about the cultural customs of the hunters of the tenth millennium B.C.E. chiefly from our discovery of killing sites, where shield-

shaped points have been found alongside mammoth bones. These points have been identified as Clovis points, named after the place in which they were first found, and their chief distinguishing feature is a groove at the base of the point that was designed to facilitate fastening it to a shaft. The most important killing sites have been unearthed in the Great Plains region (at Llanos, to be precise) and in the southwestern United States. In these territories, during the period that we are now considering, the hunters set out to catch very large game, unlike the practice that was common further east, although grooved points have been found there as well.

Additional discoveries of grooved points provides evidence that as the glaciers progressively retreated, some hunters moved northward while others move toward present-day Mexico and Central America. The elephant became extinct at the beginning of the ninth millennium B.C.E. in the Great Plains region and surrounding territories, and so the hunting peoples of this region were obliged to shift their specialization to the hunting of a type of bison that is now extinct. During the same period, we find the first examples of a stone point that is smaller than the Clovis point, featuring a grooving that almost entirely covered the surface of both faces. This was the so-called Folsom point, named after the settlement in Colorado where the first such point was unearthed along with a number of bison bones during a dig in 1926. The Folsom culture (also known as the Lindenmeier culture, from the name of the town in which the remains of a great encampment were unearthed, along with stone tools and bones embellished with carvings) lasted for roughly a thousand years.

It is believed that in what is now Mexico there were populations that were closely linked to those just described, including the Lerma culture in the central and northeastern territories and Ajuereado culture in the central territories. The remains of mammoths have been found in the Valley of Mexico, on the shores of the great lake that then existed there, and at Santa Isabel Iztapan — one of the most thoroughly studied sites — a number of points have been found along with tools that must have been used in skinning and butchering the animals. Not far from Tepexpan the skeleton of a hunter has been unearthed; a dating of 8000 B.C.E. has been suggested, but this figure is open to debate.

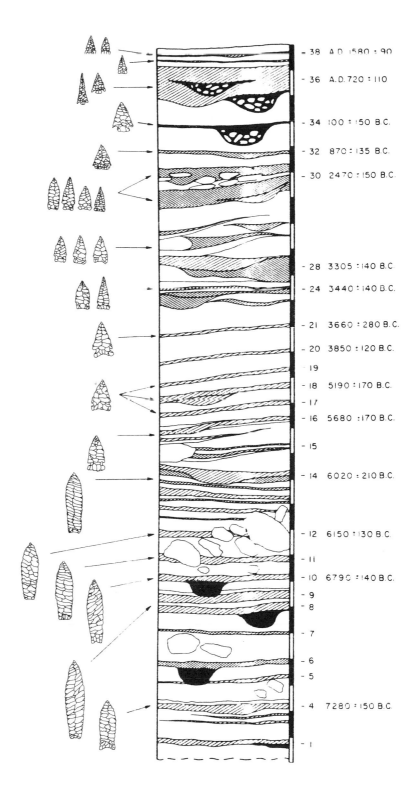

Facing page, bottom: *A group of hunters has succeeded in trapping a mammoth in a swampy area and is attacking it with spears and stones.*

Following double-page spread: *A number of hunters, disguised as reindeer, attack an isolated bison.*

Stratigraphic profile of Mummy Cave (a large rocky cavern in Wyoming, in the northwestern U.S.A.). The excavation has revealed 38 periods of human occupation separated by intervals of no occupation. The Paleo-Indian lanceolate points found here remained in use until about 6000 B.C.E.; the hunter-gatherers of later times used triangular points (with or without a side notch) and a base.

6 The First Inhabitants: Hunters and Gatherers of the Andes

THE SITUATION in South America is a bit more complex than that to the north. Archaeologists have found evidence there of the presence of many different cultural groups that flourished almost simultaneously. Around the tenth millennium B.C.E. there were a number of different technical traditions. Around the year 11,000 B.C.E. in Venezuela (at Muaco and at Taima-Taima), there lived a group of mastodon hunters who made use of fairly large lanceolate points known as El Jobo points. During the same period, in the eastern region of Brazil (at the Alice Boer site), the population began to manu-

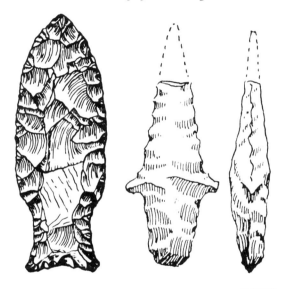

Left: *Fell-type ("fish-tail") points found in various sites in Central and South America.*
Right: *A lanceolate point with a base, found in the cavern of Lauricocha (Peru).*

A denizen of the late glacial age in far South America: the milodon. In the background, the Eberhardt cavern, also known as the Cave of the Milodon.
(Drawing and reconstruction based on the work of V. O. A. Blanch, in J. Schobinger's *Prehistoria de Sudamérica. Culturas precerámicas* [1988])

facture smaller points that featured a fastening structure at the base. Shortly thereafter, around 9300 B.C.E., the hunters of central Chile used extremely well-made stone weapons to fell mastodons, horses, and large stags along the shores of the ancient lagoon of Tagua-Tagua.

Oddly enough, the earliest clearly specialized or "higher" hunters made their first appearance in the far south of the South American continent. In five caverns in Argentina (Fell, Palli-Aike, Cueva del Medio, Los Toldos, and El Ceibo), archaeologists have conducted digs down to considerable depths. In the first three caverns they found points with "fish-tail" bases and a groove that is quite similar to that of the Clovis point. There is some uncertainty about their precise origin, but they are believed to derive in a more-or-less direct line from the Clovis point, and they have been dated roughly from 9000 or 8000 B.C.E.

The "fish-tail" points spread rapidly. They have been found in Chiapas, southern Mexico, Costa Rica, Panama, Colombia, Venezuela, and Brazil. A few have also been found at El Inga, near Quito, Ecuador, in the Andean Sierra, as well as in Peru and Uruguay. The antiquity of these latter finds has led some scholars to hypothesize that these "fish-tail" points might constitute a case of "independent creativity" that originated in the region of Pampas-Patagonia and later spread to Brazil.

The humans whose remains are found in the horizon of the paleo-American period hunted the last surviving horses to roam the steppes of Patagonia and occasionally captured milodons (a species of giant mammal belonging to the edentate order). The descendants of these hunters specialized in hunting the guanaco, a type of llama. Although these descendants left evidence of advances in the areas of technology and style, they fundamentally preserved intact the lifestyle of the Paleolithic. In the coastal strip of northern and central Peru and in a few places in Ecuador, a small number of archaeological sites have yielded rich finds of broad stone points featuring an unusual base produced by a group of hunters called the Paiján. The so-called "horizon of lanceolate points" (derived from the Venezuelan points of the El Jobo variety) dominated especially in the Andean region after around 8000 B.C.E.; the animals that roamed this area were for the most part Cervidae and Camelidae.

Among the prime Andean finds are those at Guitarrero, Quishqui Punku, Lauricocha, and Jaywamachay. Especially important is the cavern of Toquepala in southern Peru, on the walls of which rock paintings portray scenes of hunting. In the huge cavern of Inti-Huasi in the Sierra de San Luis (Argentina), a stratigraphic excavation has unearthed numerous lanceolate and leaf-shaped points dating from around 6000 B.C.E. The most recent

At the end of the Ice Age, a group of hunters armed with spears, clubs, and boleadoras (foreground left) *lays waiting in ambush for a herd of wild horses in search of water. The horse died out early and did not reappear on the continent for many millennia, when the Europeans reintroduced it to the Americas.* (Drawing by G. Gaudenzi)

studies tell us that the hunters that made use of these points often migrated southward. Fundamentally, they were not specialized hunters but rather "specialized gatherers" who adapted to the various ecosystems of the highlands and the Andean and sub-Andean valleys. In many cases, they practiced seasonal migration and led a semi-nomadic existence, hunting only during the summer and at great elevations. These groups, by the way, were the forerunners of the earliest farmers and herders of Camelidae.

Stone implements made by hunter-fishers during the second phase of the El Tunél site (Beagle Channel, Tierra del Fuego). Top: scrapers and razors; bottom: mace heads and an anvil stone. (Photograph by L. Orquera)

Paleo-Indian spear-points found in the southeastern United States. Top row, from left: *Folsom, Folsom, Sandia.* Bottom row: *Clovis, Clovis, Ventana Complex. The largest is 7 centimeters (3 inches) in length.*
(Maxwell Museum of Anthropology, Albuquerque)

Stone plow, wooden palette, and food-stuffs: maize, beans, gourd fragments, sunflower seeds, and fragments of persimmon.
(Maxwell Museum of Anthropology, Albuquerque)

Facing page: *The valley of Quereo (Chile). In the distance is the Pacific Ocean.*
(Photograph taken by the author sometime after the completion of digs in the prehistoric site, located along the left bank of the mountain stream)

7 Petroglyphic Art (Rock Painting and Sculpture)

Facing page, top: The Pinturas River in Patagonia (Argentina), seen from the interior of the Cueva de las Manos.

Bottom: Two drawings from the area of São Raimundo Nonato (northeastern Brazil). Left: a hunter with the tools of his trade (throwing stick, spears, and bag). Right: adoration of a sacred tree.
(Reproduction supervised by N. Guidon)

Page 34: A rock shelter covered with handprints, Pinturas River, Argentina.
(Photograph by G. Ligabue)

Page 35: Rock incisions belonging to various phases on a rocky wall near Monticello, Utah.
(Photograph by Anati)

SITES IN northeastern Brazil have yielded a wealth of petroglyphic art that dates from the earliest times, although we are still uncertain as to the precise chronology of the work. This art, referred to as the "Northeast Tradition," is distinguished by moderately sized figures, generally red in color, that are dynamic and naturalistic in style. The rock walls bear images of stylized human beings and animals in scenes of hunting, battle, dancing, coupling, and birth. In a few instances, geometric and symbolic figures are evident. Nière Guidon, the leading scholar working on these pictographs, believes that this style dates from between 10,000 and 5000 B.C.E., but this is strictly hypothetical.

A similar tradition, particularly with respect to the naturalistic tendency, is the "Highland Tradition," the most important examples of which have been found in the higher areas of the region of Bahía, to the east of the San Francisco River, to the west of Goiás, and southward, in the regions of São Paulo and Paraná. These paintings are dominated by figures of animals (in some cases, very large animals) free of any anthropomorphic features whatsoever. At still other sites the walls are also marked with geometric figures. It is not possible to make out any full-fledged depiction of scenes; the predominant color is red (a number of different shades), and there is a smaller presence of yellow in cases.

The paintings of the hunters of Patagonia are certainly the oldest, dating from the period of 9000 to 6000 B.C.E. These paintings have been found in a number of sites in the province of Santa Cruz (the caves of Los Toldos and El Ceibo) and in the caverns and grottoes along the Rio Pinturas. The most important motifs that recur in these sites are the figures of guanacos, often shown surrounded by figures of little men, series of points in a line, and simple geometric figures. Another motif, which is particularly striking given its parallelism with paleolithic European art, is "negative handprints," where the area surrounding the hand is colored. (These have been found in an area in the southern United States as well but have not yet been dated.)

Paintings with dynamic scenes from the cave of Xique-Xique I (Carnauba dos Dantas, Rio Grande do Norte). On the right would appear to be a depiction of the sacrifice of an animal supervised by a shaman wearing deer horns. (Based on the work of Cardich)

Right: *Violet-colored anthropomorphic figure from Cueva de las Manos, Santa Cruz, Argentina.*

Far right: *Naturalistic depictions of the region of Lagôa Santa: scenes of deer and probably a tapir (bottom).*
(Reproductions by the Franco-Brazilian Archaeological Mission)

Perhaps a common ritual, such as an initiation rite, led the humans of the paleolithic to create the same iconography; unfortunately the underlying symbolism is lost to us. Recently, paintings have been found in the negative-handprint style in Chilean Patagonia as well (in the province of Aysén).

In the area of La Martita (on the highlands of Santa Cruz), Duran has discovered a series of caverns decorated chiefly with zoomorphic motifs (figures of Camelidae), which are often covered with rocky detritus. At a distance of just seventy kilometers (43 mi.) from this zone, facing a lagoon, at the El Ccibo site, there is a complex of nine caves in a line stretching from east to west. On both of the side walls and on the innermost wall of one of these caves, there are three large stylized figures of big cats. Of the three, only one is still clearly visible: it stands a meter and a half (almost 5 ft.) tall. It is red in color, with black points on the body. Beneath this rare iconography, which may have had some association with shamanistic practices, one can see guanacos painted in white, upon which a number of handprints have been placed. These paintings have been dated to the eighth millennium B.C.E. A. Cardich, who discovered this complex of caves, claims that the big cat portrayed here is the *panthera onca mesembrina,* a variety of jaguar that became extinct at the beginning of the postglacial era.

Separate treatment should be accorded to the animalistic rock paintings containing scenes of hunting that developed in the central Andean region during the period known as the "horizon of lanceolate points." The figures are dynamic and relatively stylized. The most important site is the cave of Toquepala, in the south of Peru, which dates from 7500 B.C.E. On some of the paintings it is possible to make out small marks and scratches, which may be interpreted as traces of propitiatory rites linked to hunting.

Inside one of the caves of Sumbay (in the area around Arequipa), which was discovered and studied by M. Neira, a great many stone artifacts have been found. The walls are adorned with relatively stylized paintings of Camelidae and humans, ostriches (which have since become extinct in this area), felines, and a creature — perhaps a wizard or a deity — with the head of a bird. In contrast with other Andean sites, where the predominant color is red, white prevails at Sumbay. More similar to those other sites are the caves of Lauricocha in the Sierra Central, which are richly embellished with seminaturalistic paintings in red. These walls contain scenes of hunting and dance dating from a period in the Preceramic, that have not yet been completely identified. The territory of the Chilean Andes (the Pampa de Junín and the Cordillera de Arica) is also rich in ancient examples of rock paintings of excellent workmanship.

*Fremont-style rock incisions at Fruita Point,
Capitol Reef, southern Utah. The height of the
largest figure is about 150 centimeters (58.5 in.).*

PART II

The American Neolithic

Bowl in dyed natural fibers from the thirteenth-century Cibola region (height 25 cm./9.75 in.).
(Chamber of Commerce Museum, Grants, New Mexico)

Polished polychromatic ceramic bowl from the Pueblo IV period, mid-thirteenth-century Zuni region.
(Indian Art Fund, School of American Research, Santa Fe, New Mexico)

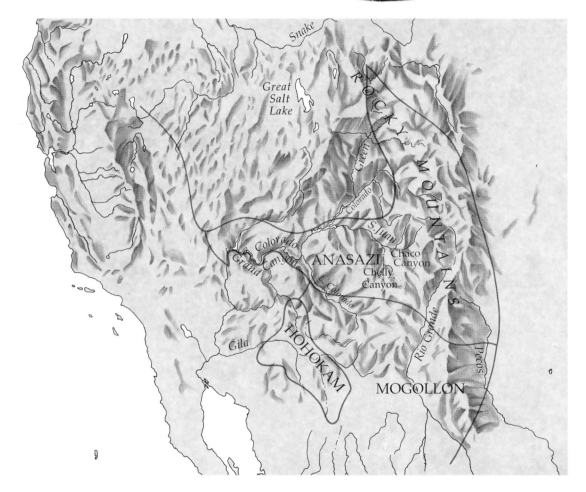

View of the White House Ruin, Canyon de Chelley, eastern Kayenta region, Arizona, eleventh-thirteenth century.
(Photograph by A. Contri)

View of Quebrada de Aguas Blancas (San Juan province) rich in stone workings and petroglyphs.

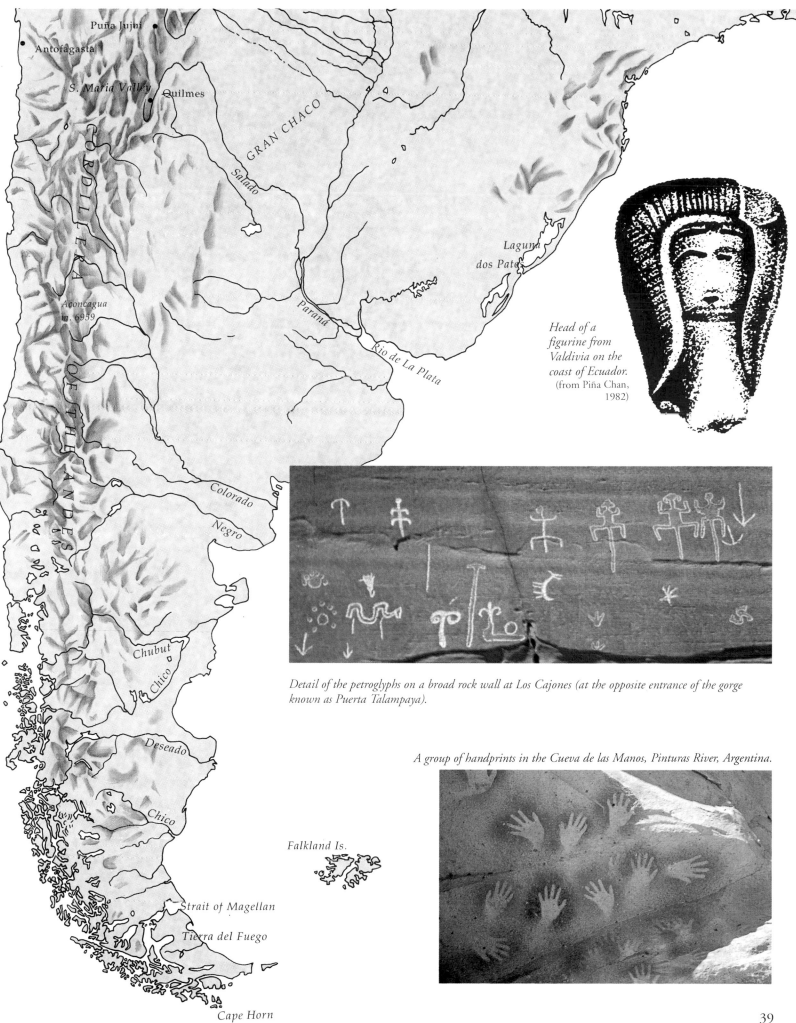

Head of a figurine from Valdivia on the coast of Ecuador.
(from Piña Chan, 1982)

Detail of the petroglyphs on a broad rock wall at Los Cajones (at the opposite entrance of the gorge known as Puerta Talampaya).

A group of handprints in the Cueva de las Manos, Pinturas River, Argentina.

1 The Earliest Farmers and Ceramists

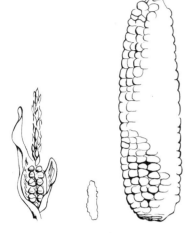

Left and center: *Two species of primitive maize, together with modern maize. The dimensions are to scale.*

(From Mangelsdorf, MacNeish, and Galinat, "Prehistoric Wild and Cultivated Maize," in *Prehistory of the Tehuacán Valley,* vol. 1 [Austin: University of Texas Press, 1967])

ACCORDING TO the findings of archaeologists and paleobotanists, the origins of American agriculture date from the seventh millennium B.C.E., the period in which the first farmers of the migratory Preceramic communities of Mexico and the central southern Andean region began seasonal cultivation of a number of wild fruit-bearing plants. The domestication of maize, more specifically, dates from the fifth millennium B.C.E., which still falls within the Preceramic period.

In the Andean region, this process began with the cultivation of different plants in regions quite distant one from another. By the seventh millennium B.C.E., beans were being cultivated in northern Peru, while a primitive variety of maize was being cultivated in the far northwestern part of Argentina. The dried remains of beans dating from about the same period were found in the rocky grotto of San Pedro Viejo de Pichasca, in the territory that the Chileans call the "Little North" (Pequeño Norte). These scattered bits of evidence allow us to conclude that a number of groups of hunter-gatherers belonging to the Andean tradition practiced a primitive form of agriculture during the intervals between their seasonal migrations. They also seem to have undertaken the breeding and keeping of livestock. Evidence from excavations performed in the Pampa de Junín in Peru suggests that by about 4500 B.C.E. there was an increasingly strong link between humans and Camelidae; two thousand years later this bond resulted in the domestication of the llama and of the alpaca.

It is interesting to note that the cultivation of maize was interrupted for a time in the southern regions, while it continued in the Peruvian Sierra. In the valleys around Ayacucho, beginning around 4000 B.C.E. (still in the Preceramic context), there was an intensification in cultivation and a diversification of the crops raised. Amaranth (an ear-bearing plant similar to primitive maize), gourds (*Cucurbitaceae),* and buckwheat made their first appearances. Another group of food plants that was destined to undergo a process of domestication was that of the tubers and rhizomes in the highland regions; these plants had already been cultivated intensively by the Preceramic Andeans, and they developed into numerous different varieties of potatoes and other local products such as añu and ullucu.

In this initial phase, agriculture extended sporadically to the coast of Peru as well. It became a permanent feature among the semi-nomadic fishing populations there by around 4000 B.C.E. At Chilca, where archaeologists have uncovered the remains of a village comprising circular huts with conical roofs and walls made of plant fibers, the inhabitants cultivated chili peppers as well as a variety of beans and gourds — the gourds being employed both as food and as containers. Given the arid climate of the zone, it is believed that the farmers took advantage of the seasonal overflow of the rivers that run down from the Cordillera to irrigate their crops.

The most important new crop introduction, which took place around 2500 B.C.E., was cotton, which developed out of a hybrid of a local plant variety with another variety that came originally

Reconstruction of one of the houses forming the ancient village of Real Alto (Ecuador), according to the excavations directed by Jorge Marcos.

from southern Asia. The arrival of this hybrid is probably best explained by a trans-Pacific contact of some sort. In any event, it marked the beginning of the development of the Peruvian textiles industry. During the same period, art developed, especially in the area of basket-making and the adornment of storage receptacles made of gourds. The lithic industry remained quite unrefined and consisted predominantly of the production of stone axes. Religion took shape in the form of complex funeral rites and, around 2000 B.C.E., in the construction of the earliest temples along the coasts and in the Sierras. Society began to organize itself into classes to some degree, as well, and an extremely influential caste of priests stood above all others.

At the same time as or prior to the Preceramic Neolithic of the Peruvian coasts (2500-1800 B.C.E.), something quite different was taking place along the coasts of Colombia and Ecuador. In this humid area, the remains of agricultural cultivation date back at least to the third millennium, a period in which the sea was one of the chief sources of food. This is the area in which ceramics first developed in the Americas. Archaeologists have found vases decorated with incisions produced by at least two cultural groups that lived in the sites of Monsù and Puerto Hormiga in northern Colombia and Valdivia along the coast of Ecuador around 3300 B.C.E. The culture of Valdivia is particularly interesting. After an initial phase of production, this

group began to produce a type of ceramic that was distinguished by the presence of a number of engraved motifs bearing many similarities to pottery produced during the same period by the Jomon culture in the southern islands of Japan. It would seem that we can safely hypothesize that new trans-Pacific contacts occurred during this period — a hypothesis that is further bolstered by the fact that the inhabitants of Valdivia were accomplished sailors.

In conjunction with the increase in trade in products of all sorts, Neolithic communities expanded and flourished, developing considerable religious activities. In the third millennium B.C.E., the first ceremonial centers were established at Valdivia, an example of which is the site of Real Alto, at a distance of about twenty kilometers (13 mi.) from the coast.

The production of ceramics continued to develop in two Ecuadorian cultures — the Machalilla (1400-1000 B.C.E.) and the Chorrera (1000-500 B.C.E.) — the latter of which is known in particular for the remarkable quality of its modeled and painted ceramics. Machalilla terracotta, on the other hand, is characterized chiefly by the presence of geometric and anthropomorphic decorations and by the introduction of a type of vase with a stirrup-shaped mouth. This type of pottery predates by a number of centuries the style found in the so-called Middle Preclassic culture of Mexico and the Middle Formative culture of Peru.

Female statuette in the distinctive Valdivia style from the "ancient formative" period of the coastal zone of Ecuador (height, 6 cm./2.4 in.).

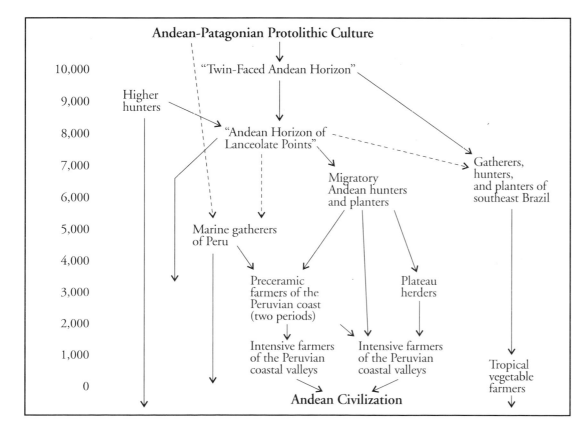

Chart of the origins and development of agriculture in South America and the probable relationships among the leading cultural groups.

Andean-Patagonian Protolithic Culture

10,000	"Twin-Faced Andean Horizon"
9,000	Higher hunters
8,000	"Andean Horizon of Lanceolate Points"
7,000	Gatherers, hunters, and planters of southeast Brazil
6,000	Migratory Andean hunters and planters
5,000	Marine gatherers of Peru
4,000	
3,000	Preceramic farmers of the Peruvian coast (two periods) — Plateau herders
2,000	
1,000	Intensive farmers of the Peruvian coastal valleys — Intensive farmers of the Peruvian coastal valleys
0	Tropical vegetable farmers

Andean Civilization

View of the Peruvian coastal desert in the vicinity of the Valley of Huarmey. In the foreground, the archaeological area of Los Gavilanes, during the dig directed by Duccio Bonavia. The round depressions correspond to the old storehouses in which maize was stored during the Preceramic period (2800 B.C.E.*).*

Facing page: *Artist's conception of the Preceramic storehouses of Los Gavilanes.*
(Drawing by Félix Caycho Quispe, based on indications given by Bonavia)

2 The Argentine Northwest

DURING THE COURSE of the second millennium B.C.E., a twofold process took place: the Neolithic way of life spread over substantial areas of the continent (especially in the northern regions of South America, in Central America, and in the eastern and southeastern sections of North America), and two specific areas developed at a very rapid pace, areas that were to become home to the more greatly evolved pre-Columbian cultures — specifically, Mesoamerica and the Central Andean Area. It has become common to designate this phase of development with the term *Formative,* inasmuch as it represents the phase of formation in the development of the two chief urban cultures that arose in both of these regions around the beginning of the Common Era.

Before we investigate these cultures further, however, we should turn our attention to two other cultural groups that developed under the influence of both the Neolithic and other nearby cultures without attaining a full-fledged level of state and urban development. The first of these groups includes the peoples of the Argentine Northwest, an area dotted with mountain valleys at the foot of the Andean Puna and Cordillera; the second group includes the peoples that inhabited part of what is now the southwestern United States. The ethnic and historic data we possess indicates that the former peoples were known as the Diaghiti, and the latter were known as the Anasazi. As we shall see, these populations shared a number of similarities — similarities that were once largely believed to be a result of a shared substrate but that are now more typically attributed to common geographic and climatic conditions and to a common proximity to the more advanced civilizations.

Scholars have divided the chronology of the Argentine Northwest into three periods: Ancient, Middle, and Late. We will look briefly at the Ancient and Late phases of the Diaghiti, but we will concentrate on the Middle period in particular, designated in archaeological terms as the culture of La Aguada, a period that has left a considerable quantity of artifacts distinguished by an extremely high level of artistic quality and having great anthropological value.

From an anthropological point of view, the region that we we are looking at forms part of the Southern Andean Area, which includes the arid and semiarid regions that now form part of Bolivia (the central and southern highlands and the eastern valleys), northern and central Chile, western and northwestern Argentina (the Puna highlands and the surrounding valleys and gorges, the Sierras of Córdoba and of San Luis, and the western provinces of San Juan and Mendoza). Evidence indicates clearly that this region was first inhabited by the Andean hunter-gatherers of the postglacial period. We have much less evidence concerning the Preceramic agricultural period. The oldest ceramics — though of more recent date than those found in Peru (1800 B.C.E.) and in the highlands of Lake Titicaca (1200 B.C.E.) — seem to have been brought from the north. The earliest Neolithic villages, with a few rare exceptions, arose in northwestern Argentina and northern Chile between 600 and 500 B.C.E.

The Argentine Northwest consists of broad valleys and gorges located at between 1,500 and 3,000 meters (5,000 to 10,000 ft.) in elevation. Annual precipitation in this zone averages around 250 millimeters (10 in.) but varies widely from one area to another, and the temperature averages about 20° Celsius (70° F.). The land supports the common vegetation of the steppe — shrubs and cactaceous plants.

Cultivation of the land was made possible through irrigation of the alluvial cones and the valley floors. The llama was a relatively easy animal to domesticate. Intense trade and communication among the valleys were not sufficient to eliminate many cultural idiosyncrasies, and yet a specific way of life did originate here, and over the course of the years cultural elements — introduced from the east through the great river basins, from the north along the trails crossing the Puna, and from the west over the mountain passes of the Cordillera of the Andes — were amalgamated and attained equilibrium.

The Campo de Pucará, one of the high valleys in the Argentine Northwest, with a herd of llamas. On the terracing in the lower valley are the ruins of La Alumbrera, from the local period of early agricultural villages. (Photograph by the author)

Landscape of the Argentine Northwest, Puna de Jujuy sector. In the foreground is a modern-day village.
(Photograph by the author)

Landscape of the Argentine Northwest. In the foreground, the ruins of village antedating the arrival of the Spaniards. (Photograph by the author)

The valley of Uspallata and the ridge of Tundqueral, Mendoza province, Argentina, a major site for rock carvings. (Photograph by the author)

Top: *The Quebrada of Inca-Cueva, Jujuy province, Argentina, with the large shelter that gives the place its name.* (Photograph by the author)

Bottom: *A series of llamas tied together with cords. Paintings from the shelter of Inca-Cueva.* (Photograph by the author)

3 The Ancient and Middle Village Period

DURING THE Ancient period, a number of different groups of farmers and llama herders settled in the Andean and sub-Andean area; others occupied what is now eastern Bolivia and the western strip of the Grand Chaco plains. Along the coast of Chile, fisherfolk and gatherers of mollusks began to integrate with the new cultures, but the peoples living in the zone of Arica failed to do the same. In the valleys of the Argentine Northwest, villages were made up of a number of habitations built to a circular plan, sometimes in scattered array and in other cases arranged in a perfect circle around a central clearing.

At Tafí, a number of monoliths, or *menhirs,* were erected, some of them smooth and others carved with patterns consisting of anthropomorphic or geometric figures that clearly had religious symbolism, comparable to those found in the temple cultures of the Middle Formative in the central and northern Andean Area. During the same period of time, a more complex variant on this type of settlement began to become common at El Alamito. This variant was connected with the spread of the two main types of ceramics dating from this period, the La Ciénaga variety (monochrome) and the Condorhuasi variety (polychrome). One particular feature — not believed to be of Andean origin — is found in both of these otherwise distinct cultures: funerary urns used in the burial of children. Along with these urns have been found the remains of decorated pipes that were used to ingest hallucinogenic substances for ritual purposes. The sites have also yielded evidence of primitive gold and copper working.

The social system of this period was that of the "autonomous village," in which the shaman exercised enormous influence, as we can see from the symbols contained in rock carvings and drawings.

The cultures of the Middle period, while not showing any substantial technical or economic shifts relative to the Ancient period, do reflect the influence of the religious center of Tiahuanaco. One example can be seen at San Pedro de Atacama in northern Chile, where artifacts have been found that were made from perishable materials, including clothing, flutes, pottery, and wooden artifacts. Shiny black ceramics with geometric engravings have also been found at this site.

The influence of Tiahuanaco reached as far as the Argentine Northwest, where it engendered the culture of La Aguada, which in turn attained the highest level of artistic expression in the area. The heads of the social structure in that culture were the warrior-priests, who sometimes played the role of "sacrificers." The state of trance that these warrior-priests regularly attained during ceremonies was symbolized in the culture's art by a dragon-shaped feline that was often associated with other naturalistic motifs.

The earliest attempts in this area to cast bronze also date from this period. The alloy was used for the first time by the inhabitants of Tiahuanaco. La Aguada was the first site to produce ceremonial structures with a pyramidal shape, made up of three platforms and an access ramp, set before a rectangular plaza. The area's earliest fortresses appeared on the surrounding hills.

The villages of La Aguada were generally made up of a number of dwellings (typically five to ten) set close to one another on a circular or an oval plan, usually in the middle of the cultivated fields. The economy must have been primarily based upon agriculture. Maize was cultivated, and the diet was filled out with wild fruit, especially carobs, and with the meat of Camelidae. Among the most distinctive surviving artifacts are cylindrical vases decorated with figures of big cats and warriors carrying axes and heads as trophies; also noteworthy are collared

Below left: Depictions of human beings engraved on ceramic objects from La Aguada, Argentina (according to Serrano).

Right: The "dragon-shaped feline" in a number of variations, painted on pottery from the culture of La Aguada (according to Serrano).

axes, mortars, and millstones used to grind grains and cereals and to prepare vegetable dyes. The few objects that were made of bone were for the most part used in the fabrication of textiles. There were also very few artifacts made of wood. What is perhaps most striking in terms of the iconography involved in the depiction of human figures, whether painted or sculpted, are the extremely elaborate hairstyles and the ornamentations that appear on the foreheads. Both these forms of adornment were closely linked to one's position in the social hierarchy. Tattooing and face-painting were both common practices, as was the use of earrings and pectorals. Ceramics attained very high levels of quality. Decorations were polychrome, in three or four colors. One quite common and distinctive form of pottery featured a shiny orange or dark brown color with an extremely fine impasto engraved with geometric motifs or with stylized figures of felines. The most common forms of receptacles were tall and cylindrical, truncated cone-shaped, hourglass shaped with half-ring handles, globular, and subglobular.

Additionally the people produced anthropomorphic statuettes that were reddish-yellow in color and pipes decorated with feline shapes and monstrous figures depicted in relief. Their bronze work included axes made in the shape of a T and adorned with feline shapes, agricultural implements, ornaments to be worn on the forehead, tweezers for plucking hairs, bracelets, and earrings. A number of surviving pectorals provide evidence of remarkable workmanship; these artifacts typically depict a central figure with stylized felines on either side. One noteworthy example of this is the "disk of Lafone-Quevedo," now in the collection of the Museum of La Plata. The central figure in this disk has a single large eye from which rays are emanating upward. The feline symbol (either panther or jaguar) played a fundamental role in the indigenous belief system. The basic symbol was elaborated into a number of different forms, such as that of a reptile with hands and feet, the head of a monstrous creature, a man, a bird, or even a dragon.

Graves were typically oval or circular in shape or, less frequently, rectangular or square. They tended to be two or three meters (7 to 10 ft.) in depth and to be plotted together in full-fledged cemeteries. Burial took place in a number of different ways. Children, for example, were buried directly in the ground, and, although a number of collective burial places have been found, graves were largely individual. The deceased was buried in the fetal position, oriented from north to south, with the head leaning on the shoulder as if looking upward. The funerary furnishings varied greatly in quantity and quality, which would seem to point to a clear social and political hierarchy, in the context of which warriors enjoyed promi-

nent superiority. It is also possible to hypothesize the presence of a head-trophy cult (a number of isolated skulls have been found in graves) and the practice of human sacrifice.

The essential origins of La Aguada have been traced to the cultures of La Ciénaga, Condorhuasi, El Alamito, and, at a greater remove, that of Tiahuanaco. Some additional features (the "sacrificer," the cult of the head trophies, the ceremonial axes) originated in the north and came to La Aguada through the Chilean Puna, undergoing slight mutations in the process. The culture of La Aguada fell into decline in the ninth century B.C.E. as the cultural influx from the area around Lake Titicaca diminished and the influx of peoples from the Amazon basin increased. With the decline of La Aguada, the image of the dragon-shaped feline lost its symbolic value and became nothing more than a decorative form.

The "human-feline": a rock painting from the major shamanistic-ceremonial center of La Tunita, near Ancasti, east of Catamarca, Argentina. Based on a copy made by N. de la Fuente.

Monolithic carved figure found in the "corridor" running between the stone structures and the platform of Unit B at the archaeological site of El Alamito (width, 98 cm./39 in.).

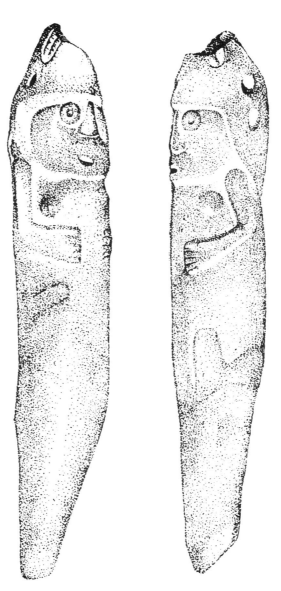

Painted vase from La Aguada, with a stylized bird motif.
(Museum of La Plata)

Black ceramics, with engraved geometric decoration, from the culture of La Ciénaga (approximately 0 to 600 C.E.).
(Museum of La Plata)

Bowl with an engraving depicting the "dragon-shaped feline" of the culture of La Aguada (ca. 600-900 C.E.).
(Museum of La Plata)

Black ceramics engraved with geometric motifs and schematic human faces from the culture of La Ciénaga. (Museum of La Plata)

51

4 The Late Village Period

FOLLOWING A little-understood period of transition during which groups of settlers migrated from the tropical forests, a number of local cultures arose that have been given the name of "bearer peoples."

The development that occurred during this period was the result not only of an increase in the density of the population, which tended to gather in centers or semiurban concentrations that often were fortified (the so-called *pucará*) but also derived from a general evolution in agricultural and irrigation techniques, from a far stronger social hierarchy, and from an improvement in bronze metallurgy, which led to an increase in the production of tools, weapons, and ritual and funerary objects. Where ceramics is concerned, the funerary urns for children became quite widespread once again (the "Santa Maria" urns are outstanding examples). The long mouth of this sort of urn is typically decorated with an extremely stylized human face, along with geometric and zoomorphic figures (two-headed serpents, batrachians of all sorts, ostriches) and humans wearing loose-fitting tunics. A *puco* (dipper) painted with geometric motifs was used to close the urn.

The language of the prehistoric Diaghiti was *kakán,* only a few words and name places of which have survived. The most important group of this population was the Calchaquiés, who lived in the valley of the same name, in the province of Salta and, further south, in the valley of Santa María.

Each valley had a political structure not unlike that of the late medieval seigniories of Europe. The most important settlements were those of Pucará de Tilcara, Tastil, Fuerte Quemada, and Quilmes, all of which were centers in which a sort of intensive agriculture was practiced, as is attested by the remains of canals and manmade ponds also associated with cultivated areas in Peru and elsewhere. The classic Andean crops were raised there: corn, beans, gourds, and peanuts, but also potatoes and quinoa. The diet was supplemented by wild fruit and seeds.

The Diaghiti were also familiar with a number of medicinal herbs that are still in use among the natives of this region today. They raised llamas, hunted guanacos, vicuñas, and nandus (South American ostriches), and carried on some limited trading. During the Late period, rock painting and carving was still fairly popular; nonetheless, it is quite difficult to establish chronological identities among the various petroglyphs that can still be seen on the rock walls of this area, since it is rare for the iconographic motifs to coincide with the motifs used on objects in common or ceremonial use.

During this period, the Incas extended their rule for a number of decades (approximately from 1475 to 1535) to the northern and northwestern sections of modern-day Argentina and to the north and central sections of modern-day Chile. This extension of the Incan imperial system did not involve major changes for the local communities in these areas,

however. The Incas built their roads at a considerable distance from the main Diaghite settlements. They were chiefly interested in maintaining exclusive control over the mines and in securing an opportunity to trade with Chile, which was particularly rich in minerals and foodstuffs. The most important Incan ruins in this area can still be seen at Collasuyo, where a number of sanctuaries were built at an altitude ranging from 4,800 to 6,700 meters (15,750 to 22,000 ft.). Among other locations, we should mention Cerro del Plomo (5,400 m./17,712 ft.) in Central Chile, Cerro del Toro (6,250 m./20,500 ft.) and Cerro Aconcagua (5,300 m./17,384 ft.) in Argentina. At these sites remains have been found that suggest the sacrifice of infants and children during the course of the Incan rites known as *Capacocha*. The deceased were buried along with lavish funerary offerings, such as gold statuettes and Spondylus-type shells. A number of sites have yielded statuettes that were evidently used as offerings in place of human sacrifices. Following the arrival of Francisco Pizarro, the Spanish conqueror of Peru, and the fall of the Incan empire, the cultures of this zone survived for a period but declined definitively in the sixteenth century, with the foundation of the earliest Spanish colonial cities.

Paintings from the Quebrada of Durazno, Loconte, in the region of the Valley of Hualfín, Catamarca, featuring a man with a shield-shaped tunic and other figures.

53

Top: *Wall engraving at Antofagasta de la Sierra (Puna of Catamarca, Argentina), depicting a shield-shaped anthropomorphic figure seated upon a llama and a large human figure.*
(Photograph by the author)

Above, left: *Funerary urn for a child, with a relief of a human face, probably the deceased. This urn belongs to the Belén variety, from the Argentine Northwest.*
Right: *Two men are shown engraving and painting figures of guanacoes at Taira, in the valley of the river Loa in northern Chile.*
(From a reconstruction at the Chilean Museum of Pre-Columbian Art, Santiago)

Top: *Geometric paintings from Cueva Rodonda (Eastern puna of Jujuy, Argentina).* (Photograph by the author)

Bottom: *Cueva Pintada in Salta province, Argentina, featuring figures wearing ample shield-shaped tunics.* (Photograph by M. Cigliano)

5 The Southwestern United States

Reed figurine of an animal, from the Ancient period, Grand Canyon, Arizona (height, 13 cm./5 in.).
(School of American Research, Santa Fe, New Mexico)

"The Maze," Colorado River, south-eastern Utah.
(Photograph by Dudley W. King)

THE CENTRAL CORE of the area designated as the Southwestern United States is constituted by Arizona and New Mexico. The western border runs along the valley of the Colorado River, curving slightly eastward to include the southernmost extremity of Nevada as well. To the north this central core includes the southern two-thirds of Utah and the western and southwestern sections of Colorado; to the east, it includes almost all of New Mexico and a small portion of Texas; to the south, it includes the Mexican state of Sonora and almost all of Chihuahua. The culture in this territory was primarily agricultural, unlike the adjacent territories to the west and the north. Only to the south does this area border on another aboriginal agricultural area, which, as we shall see, was the largest Mesoamerican agricultural center.

In general, the climate of the southwest is dry, and it has been that way since the end of the glacial era (5000 to 2500 B.C.E.), excepting variations introduced by epicycles of erosion and sedimentation in the valley bottoms. Local differences in climate and ecosystems dictated by the altitude of the land served to provide a substantial variety of environments for the ancient inhabitants of this area, but for the most part they all experienced brief winters marked by sudden thunderstorms, lengthy summers marked by intermittent rainfall, and very dry seasons in between the two.

The region is crossed by many rivers, such as the Colorado (and its tributaries the Gila, the Little Colorado, and the San Juan) and the Rio Grande (and its tributaries the Pecos and the Texas). Ranged between these great river basins are many mountains and highlands, valleys and canyons. The canyons in particular have produced a number of important archaeological sites, including the high Rio Zuñi, Canyon de Chelly, Chaco Canyon, and Frijoles Canyon.

Anthropologists have identified three basic cultural areas in the Southwestern United States: the Anasazi to the north, the Hohokam to the southwest, and the Mogollon to the southeast. The groups arose out of a single prehistoric tradition, known as the Culture or Tradition of the Desert, which lasted until 7000 B.C.E. but subsequently differentiated in part because of differences in local geography and climate.

The shift from the relatively humid climate of the Pleistocene to the semiarid climate of the present caused a shift in living conditions among the Epipaleolithic peoples that lived in the region. The various groups adapted to this new environment in much the same thing way as the inhabitants of the central regions of Mexico did: they began to gather plants and to hunt smaller animals (rodents, foxes, and birds), adapting as well as possible to the necessary exploitation of favorable ecological niches. One of their principal strategies for survival was a shift from the ancient nomadism of the Paleolithic to a pattern of seasonal migrations. During this phase, in a number of southern regions such as Tehuacán and Tamaulipas, the earliest experiments in cultivating and domesticating plants were undertaken. Around 2000 B.C.E., a number of groups in the region were already cultivating maize, which was probably imported from areas further to the south. There is also evidence of a Preceramic cultivation of beans and various types of gourds. *Metates* (relatively flat stones well suited to grinding) came into use for the preparation of plants, and techniques for weaving and basket-making were developed. The *atlatl*, or throwing stick, was the weapon most commonly used in hunting, together with various types of stone projectiles. These groups kept no livestock; the only domesticated animals were the dog and the turkey.

An atlatl, *or throwing stick, which made it possible to throw spears with greater power and accuracy than was possible by hand.*

Rock paintings in the Great Gallery, Horseshoe Canyon, Lance National Park, southern Utah. The large figure of a shaman is about 3 meters (10 ft.) tall. These paintings would seem to date from the Archaic period, around 1000 B.C.E..
(From J. J. Brody, Anasazi, 1990)

Alamo Canyon, Pajarito highlands, northern New Mexico.
(Photograph by Dudley W. King)

Following double-page spread: *View of the Canyon de Chelley, a major center for rock paintings and carvings in northeastern Arizona.*
(Photograph by A. Contri)

6 The Ancient Hohokam, Mogollon, and Anasazi

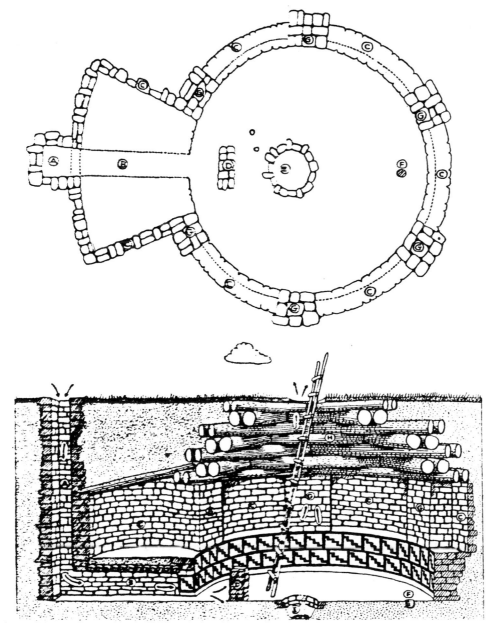

THE NAME *Hohokam* in the Pima tongue (the modern-day language of the descendants of this cultural group) means "ancient people." Around 300 B.C.E., the Hohokam began to construct fairly large villages, expanding their agriculture through the use of irrigation techniques. Archaeological evidence uncovered at the site of Snaketown in the Gila River valley, not far from the city of Phoenix, Arizona, indicates four chief phases of the Hohokam culture: Pioneer (300 B.C.E.–500 C.E.), Colonial (500-900 C.E.), Sedentary (900-1100 C.E.), and Classical (1100-1300 C.E.).

During the Pioneer period, the Hohokam lived in small villages, collections of huts made of plant fibers and clay. They practiced agriculture and were familiar with irrigation techniques. Besides ceramics, they made fabrics and constructed various forms of ornamentation out of shells.

During the Colonial period, the population grew considerably, and new settlements spread to the mountains and highlands of central and eastern Arizona. Social life became more complex, and craftsmanship became far more varied. During later periods, the villages became larger, although overall the Hohokam territory declined in size.

In a number of communities of the Classical period, such as that of Casas Grandes in Arizona, multi-storied buildings were erected using large blocks of adobe (sun-dried brick) and stones. A high rectangular wall surrounded each village. The Hohokam also had a ritual architecture, including large community houses, enclosures in which to play pelota (a court game of Mesoamerican origin), and truncated pyramids, which may well have been platforms for temples.

In some cases the ceramic objects of the Sedentary period present stylized forms of animals and birds; the decorations are typically either geometric, with spirals and undulating shapes, or else naturalistic, featuring figures of birds and small feathered humans. The most common artifacts of the Colonial and Sedentary periods are pestles, stone vases, and rectangular and rhomboid spatulas, probably used in the preparation of narcotic and psychotropic substances. During the Classical period, a group of Anasazi migrated to this region and influenced it considerably. The Hohokam erected the characteristic walls around their villages as defenses against incursions by groups from the south and Apache raiding parties (by this time the Apaches ranged the land between the region of the Athabascos in Canada and the Southwest). It is unclear whether it was external pressures of this sort or perhaps a shift in the climate that caused the Hohokams to abandon their villages during the fourteenth and fifteenth centuries.

The Mogollon area takes its name from the Mogollon mountains, which extend from central and eastern Arizona all the way to southern New Mexico. This elevated area is wetter than the surrounding desert regions, which made it possible to cultivate maize there from 2000 B.C.E. onward; crops of beans and edible gourds were added to the local diet after seeds reached the area from Mesoamerica after 1000 B.C.E. The sedentary way of life began here long before it did in the more northern areas. Ceramics appeared around 300 B.C.E., at first unadorned. Semi-subterranean structures produced during this phase can be seen at the Pine Lawn site. These houses typically feature an approximately circular floor plan, an entrance corridor, and stone pillars supporting the walls and the conical roofs.

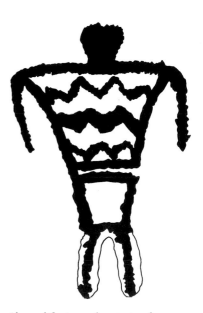

Later, there was a transition to houses with rectangular shapes built entirely above ground and — especially in the valley of Mimbres — enclosed villages. The ceramics produced in this valley were painted with refined naturalistic subjects, while in other areas the ceramics feature rectilinear and curvilinear shapes in black on a white background, showing clear Anasazi influence.

Much like the Hohokam peoples, most of the Mogollon abandoned their villages between 1100 and 1300 C.E. The only exception was that of groups living near the Rio Grande, who integrated with Pueblo villages in a later period.

Anasazi, meaning "ancient enemies," was the name given by the Navajo (who migrated from the northern section of what is now the United States around the tenth century C.E.) to the first people they met when they reached the southwest. The territory of the Anasazi was centered in the area where the borders of Colorado, Utah, Arizona, and New Mexico now meet.

Here, too, the history begins with a shift from the Preceramic Late period (the Archaic period) to the beginnings of what is known as the Basket Maker culture. Very little is known about the first phase of this period. The second phase, on the other hand, began around the same time as the Common Era and lasted about four centuries. Ceramics had yet to be discovered, but the production of baskets and associated artifacts such as receptacles, mats, and sandals had become rich and varied. The Anasazi houses were similar to those of the Mogollon: circular, semi-subterranean, and built in groups on the terraces and slopes of valleys. Storehouses for foodstuffs, on the other hand, were typically built up against canyon walls. Maize was generally cultivated (in diverse varieties) as were edible gourds.

Shamanistic rites were common, as attested by the discovery of many kinds of tubular pipes and rock paintings, especially near the Colorado River in Utah.

The third phase of the Basket Maker period (400-700 G.E.) is characterized by several developments. The group began to cultivate beans and raise turkeys. Ceramics featuring very simple decorations began to play some of the roles previously filled by baskets. Halfway through the phase, bows and arrows, stone axes, and cotton clothing made their first appearances. The villages became larger, and the houses took on a more-or-less rectangular shape with an entrance hall. One interesting example of this new type of house can be found in the village of Shabik'eshchee in northwestern New Mexico, which contains eighteen dwellings, varying in diameter from three to seven meters (10 to 23 ft.), a great many circular storehouses dug out of the earth, a *kiva* (a ceremonial circular enclosure with stone walls, the direct forerunner of the kivas of the Pueblo Indians) some twelve meters (40 ft.) in diameter, a courtyard in front of the kiva, and two great refuse dumps, or mounds. The entire complex was approximately semi-circular and opened eastward. The deceased were buried in a hunched over position, with a very scanty array of grave goods. All this suggests that there was little social stratification in the group.

Almost life-size rock painting from eastern Utah. The figure seems to be wearing decorated clothing. Attributed to the Basketmaker III period (approximately 400-700), according to Brody.

Following pages: *Sandals made of plaited fibers from the San Juan region. Approximate length 25 centimeters (10 in.). From southern Utah, a sack made of dyed hand-plaited fibers and sewn weasel skin showing original repairs. Both objects belong to the Basketmaker II period (approximately 200-400).*

(Laboratory of Anthropology, Museum of New Mexico, Santa Fe)

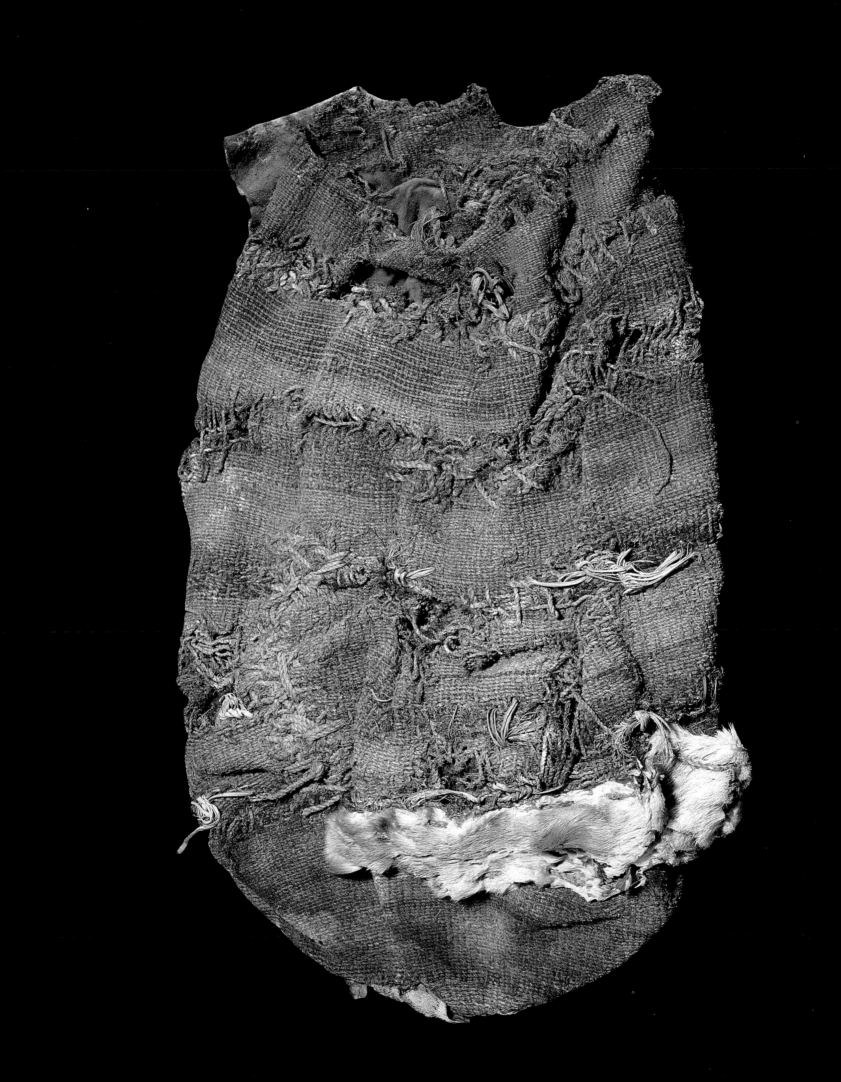

7 Anasazi-Pueblo

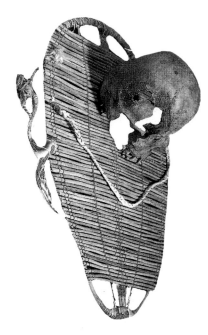

Reconstruction of a portable cradle from the Pueblo II period made of canes attached to a wooden framework. Approximate length, 70 centimeters (28 in.). The cranium belonged to an adult woman.

A newborn child bound to a portable cradle.

AROUND 700 B.C.E., another change occurred in Anasazi territory that signaled the beginning of the Pueblo period, which has survived to modern times. (The term *Pueblo* was given by Spaniards in the sixteenth century to the indigenous peoples that they plundered so regularly.) The Pueblo period comprises two phases. The first phase (700-900 C.E.) was transitional: the semi-subterranean dwellings were still present, but they were increasingly built against the sides of valley slopes. The main new development of this phase was religious. The skulls of newborns were artificially deformed by compressing their heads against their cradles. This custom was more typically Andean than Mesoamerican, had a shamanistic origin, and was connected with the growing importance of the kiva as the chief site of male initiation rites and trance rituals. The second Pueblo phase (900-1100 C.E.) was marked by the construction of true villages. This led to a considerable increase in population and to the concentration of families into groups, which in turn produced the first hierarchical societies directed by priests, who lived in the kivas. The kivas were built almost completely underground during this period, as if to protect them from evil influence. Ceramics decorated with black-on-white backgrounds first appeared during this period, as did clay jars with handles. The swift and ubiquitous spread of the various types of ceramics suggests that there were constant contacts and exchanges among the villages,

even when — later on — sizable groups headed off southward and eastward, reaching as far as the upper Pecos River.

By the end of the second Pueblo phase, the characteristic aspects of Anasazi culture were established. The people lived in large villages of buildings stacked one atop the other, the kiva and the associated shamanistic-ceremonial lifestyle were central, and there was considerable production of ceramics with stylized naturalistic and geometric decorations and with generally black patterns on a white background.

There followed a third Pueblo phase (1050-1300 C.E.), also called the "Classical" or "Great Epoch" period. During this phase the villages took on many aspects of proto-cities: there were great agglomerations of persons living in planned complexes, stone defensive fortifications, and a considerably advanced architecture. There were two principal kinds of settlements: one type of villages was built in flatlands or on the edge of valleys, and the other was set within great sheltering structures and against rocky walls (cliff dwellings). The most important example of the first type of village can be found in Chaco Canyon in the San Juan River basin in northwestern New Mexico, now a national archaeological monument.

Near the rocky cliff walls lining this valley, along a thirty-kilometer (20-mi.) stretch, there is a series of twelve semicircular villages, each bounded by a

Reconstruction of Pueblo Bonito at Chaco Canyon, as it must have looked around 1100.

(Painted by Lloyd Towsend for *Reader's Digest*)

wall open toward the river bank. A network of paths and trails linked the villages and connected them all with other, more distant villages.

The architectural style features houses made of masonry, built up a number of stories with setbacks, and terracing designed to take advantage of the sun's heat. In some of the villages there were a great number of enclosures, inside of which were smaller kivas. A larger kiva was set at the middle of the large central plaza and unquestionably constituted the main center of religious and political life. One example of this can be found at Pueblo Bonito, which, with its eight hundred enclosures, is the largest village in Chaco Canyon. It was built in three stages between 920 and 1130 C.E. All told, Chaco Canyon housed at least six thousand individuals and lay at the center of a complex economic, political, and ritual system.

The peasants, who lived in a few houses on the outskirts of the village, worked at cultivating the fields with a complex system of irrigation. Social organization was so stratified as to constitute something very close to a state. Numerous archaeological finds have established the fact that the level of artistry in this culture was particularly elevated. Recovered artifacts include turquoise inlay, copper rattles, and necklaces composed of no fewer than 5,700 seashells pierced with hardwood awls. Not much is known about the clothing these people wore, but the few surviving examples are constructed with taste and skill.

The group's ceramics also give evidence of high levels of artistry. In addition to the characteristic decoration of ceramic objects with white on a black background, red and black on an orange background came into use as well. The geometry of the decorative motifs was particularly complex, and the shapes of the pottery itself quite varied. (Some of the vases were shaped like ducks.)

A well-known example of the second kind of settlement (cliff dwellings) is that of Cliff Palace at Mesa Verde, Colorado. Here the residences were stacked one atop the other against the rear wall of a huge natural niche that formed along a sandstone cliff. A number of the houses were multistoried. Twenty-three kivas and a number of towers (probably built for defensive purposes) complete this spectacular site.

Evidence gathered from the study of tree rings indicates that a great drought hit the area at the end of the thirteenth century and lasted for twenty years, dealing a harsh blow to life in Chaco Canyon. The cities in this and other areas were largely abandoned. Around 1300, a fourth Pueblo phase began. The Anasazi concentrated in great villages, but the geographic area in which they lived shrank considerably to zones near the Little Colorado River and the Rio Grande. A few groups, such as the Hopi and Zuñi, survived until colonial times.

In 1540, the earliest Spanish expedition, under the command of Francisco Vásquez de Coronado, passed through Zuñi territory. It is believed that at that time between fifty and a hundred thousand Anasazi lived there. Colonization and missionary work in what is now New Mexico began around 1600 and marked the beginning of a fifth Pueblo phase, which has been documented not only by archaeological but also by ethnohistorical and ethnographic means. In the years that followed, the Pueblo culture declined in importance but nevertheless managed to survive. Today traditional crafts and tourism provide a subsistence living for this people in places such as Taos, New Mexico.

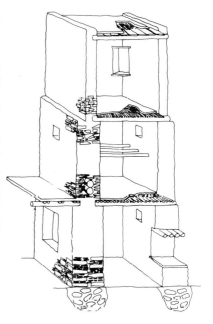

Drawing showing the Chaco method of making houses with several stories.

Following double-page spread: *Reconstruction of an Anasazi village.*

Part of a Hopi village, which still had a pre-Hispanic population at the end of the nineteenth century.
(Photograph by John Hilliers, ca. 1880)

Drawing of a temple.
Detail of a mural at Tetitla, Teotihuacan.
(Drawing by Miguel Covarrubias)

PART III

The First Metropolis: Teotihuacán

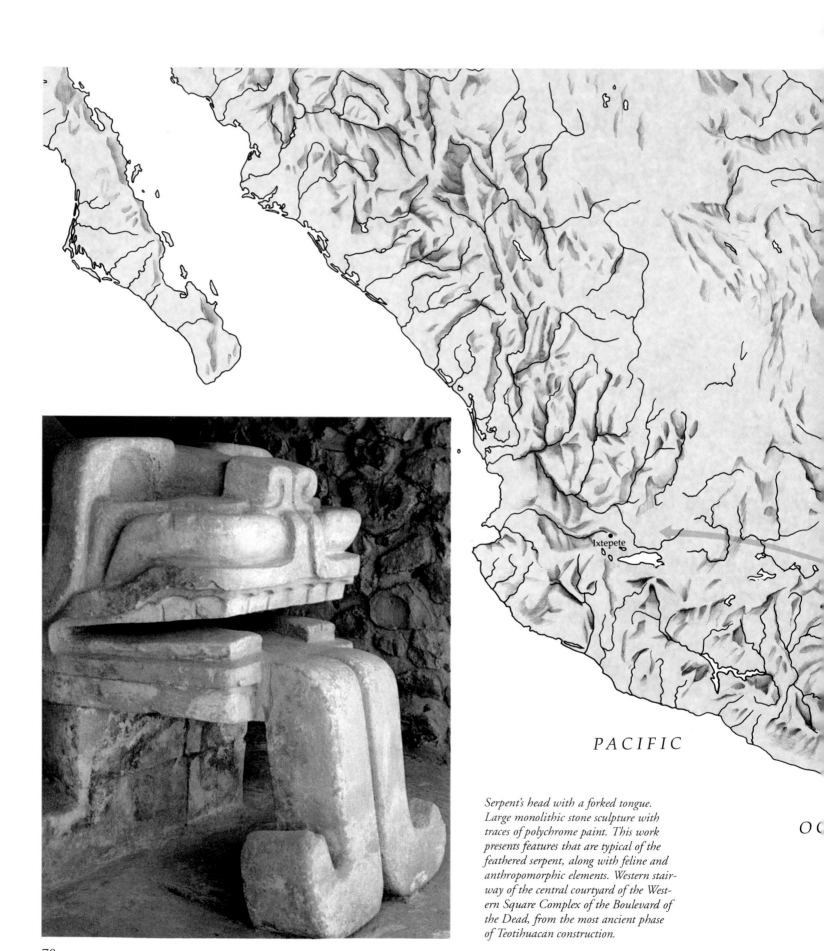

Ixtepete

PACIFIC

OC

*Serpent's head with a forked tongue.
Large monolithic stone sculpture with
traces of polychrome paint. This work
presents features that are typical of the
feathered serpent, along with feline and
anthropomorphic elements. Western stairway of the central courtyard of the Western Square Complex of the Boulevard of
the Dead, from the most ancient phase
of Teotihuacan construction.*

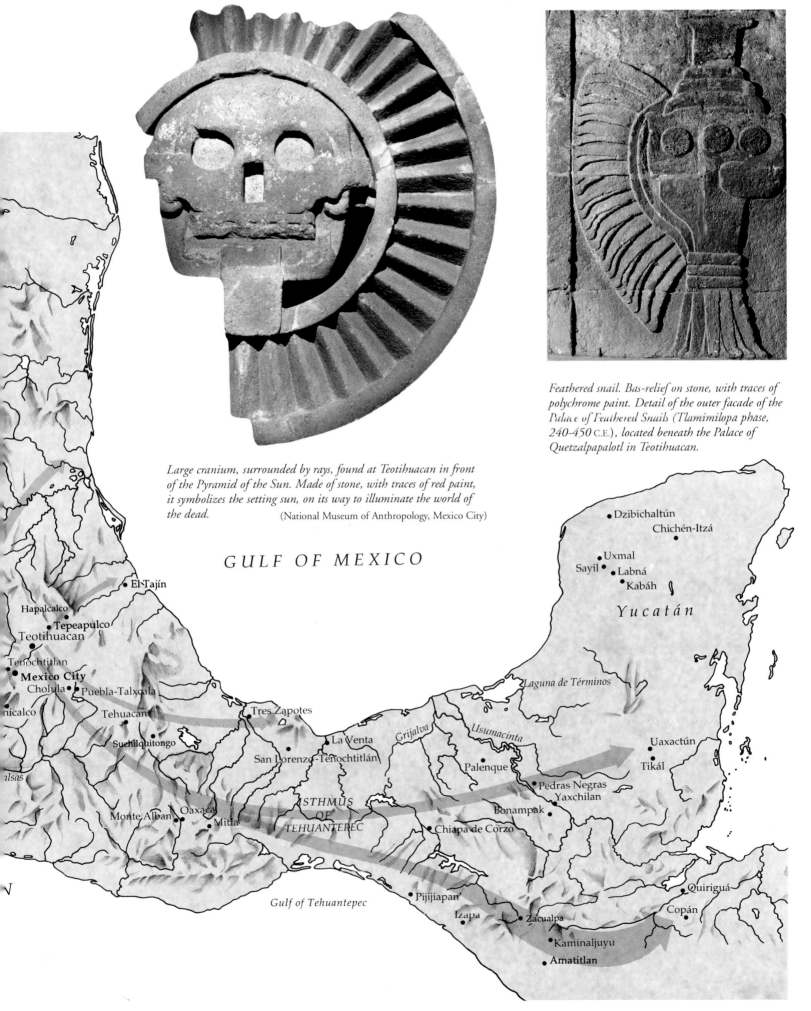

Large cranium, surrounded by rays, found at Teotihuacan in front of the Pyramid of the Sun. Made of stone, with traces of red paint, it symbolizes the setting sun, on its way to illuminate the world of the dead.
(National Museum of Anthropology, Mexico City)

Feathered snail. Bas-relief on stone, with traces of polychrome paint. Detail of the outer facade of the Palace of Feathered Snails (Tlamimilopa phase, 240-450 C.E.), located beneath the Palace of Quetzalpapalotl in Teotihuacan.

GULF OF MEXICO

El Tajín

Hapalcalco
Tepeapulco
Teotihuacan
Tenochtitlan
Mexico City
Cholula
Puebla-Talxcala
nicalco
Tehuacan
Suchilquitongo
alsas
Monte Alban
Oaxaca
Mitla
Tres Zapotes
La Venta
San Lorenzo-Tenochtitlán
ISTHMUS OF TEHUANTEPEC
Grijalva
Usumacinta
Laguna de Términos
Yucatán
Dzibichaltún
Chichén-Itzá
Uxmal
Sayil
Labná
Kabáh
Palenque
Pedras Negras
Yaxchilan
Bonampak
Chiapa de Corzo
Uaxactún
Tikál
Quiriguá
Copán
Gulf of Tehuantepec
Pijijiapan
Izapa
Zacualpa
Kaminaljuyu
Amatitlan

1 Geography and Natural Regions

WHAT IS COMMONLY referred to as Mesoamerican culture was spread over two large geographical areas. The first, which we will be examining in the following pages, took in Central Mexico and the city of Teotihuacán; the second, which we will examine further in Part IV, took in regions located further southeast and the area of the Maya. There are significant geographic and climatic differences between these to areas, but they also share a number of features.

The Mesoamerican area extends from central Honduras, western Nicaragua, and the extreme northwestern portion of Costa Rica, all the way up to the river Soto la Marina in the Mexican state of Tamaulipas and to the river Fuerte in Sinaloa.

This area supports substantial geophysical, climatic, and vegetational variations. To the north are the semiarid mountain chains of the western and eastern Sierra Madre, divided by a semidesert highland. To the south is the volcanic region of central Mexico, dotted with water basins at high altitudes and the remains of lakes dating from the Pleistocene. The southern Sierra, an intricate network of mountain chains and valleys, winds from Jalisco to Oaxaca. Beyond the isthmus of Tehuantepéc stretch the regions of Chiapas and Guatemala. The Pacific coastal region features narrow plains that run from the mountains down to the sea; the Atlantic coastal region is covered with savannah and lush tropical forests.

The climate of Mesoamerica is fundamentally tropical, though at higher elevations both temperatures and rainfall levels are far lower. Areas to the south and the east receive heavy precipitation and support a lush and abundant vegetation. Indigenous peoples employ traditional *quema y roza* (slash-and-burn) techniques to clear the land for cultivation. By contrast, the northern and western areas are arid, most especially so in the northwest. Aboriginal agriculture in this region is limited to irrigated oases.

Between these two extreme points of the region, there are the basins and high valleys of central Mexico, the southern Sierra, and the highlands of Chiapas and Guatemala. Here rainfall is moderate, the soil is fertile, and vegetation is relatively abundant — all factors that have led to intensive agriculture and a population density that is far greater than in other regions.

The cultural tradition of Mesoamerica is based on agriculture and originated around 2000 B.C.E. with the development of sedentary farming villages. Over time, this culture developed its own characteristic features and imported some elements from other cultures. It reaches its apex in the early centuries of the Common Era, although certain advanced

Chronology of archaeological cultures of Mesoamerica.

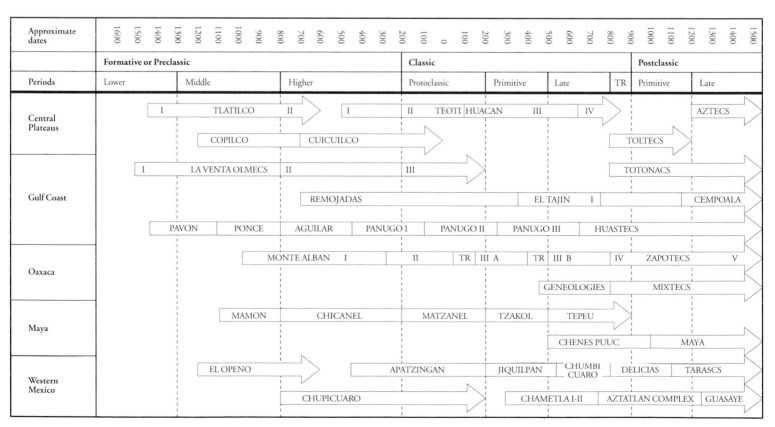

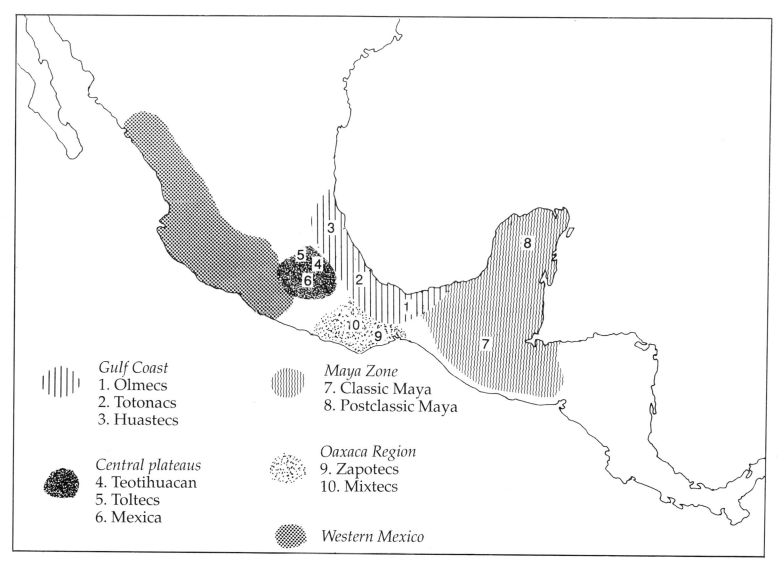

Gulf Coast
‖‖‖	1. Olmecs
	2. Totonacs
	3. Huastecs

Central plateaus
4. Teotihuacan
5. Toltecs
6. Mexica

Maya Zone
7. Classic Maya
8. Postclassic Maya

Oaxaca Region
9. Zapotecs
10. Mixtecs

Western Mexico

The archaeological-cultural areas of Mesoamerica.

technological developments — such as metallurgy — were assimilated later still.

Three zones in the central region are particularly important: the central highlands (south of Hidalgo, the Valley of Mexico, and Morelos); the valley of Puebla, Tlaxcala, and Tehuacán; and the central region of Oaxaca. Each has a climate especially favorable for farming — and, indeed, these areas sustained the development of the earliest agriculture in Mesoamerica and in all of the northern hemisphere.

When Europeans arrived in the sixteenth century, all economic and social power was concentrated in this region, and for that reason it was the first to be subjugated and colonized. Even now this region is the political, economic, and cultural heart of Mexico. It is also here that some of the most fascinating pre-Columbian ruins in the entire region have been found.

Two areas in which Mesoamerican culture typically flourished.
This page: *The ceremonial center of Paleque, immersed in the forest of Chiapas.*
Facing page: *The ceremonial center of Yagul, in the semiarid region of Oaxaca.* (Photograph by A. Maffeis)

2 The History of the Research

THE EARLIEST archaeological find of any importance took place in colonial times in the region of central Mexico: the famous "Sun Stone," an Aztec calendar, was unearthed in the central plaza of Mexico City, in 1790. This stone disk, measuring 3.6 meters (almost 12 ft.) in diameter bears all of the principal symbols of Aztec cosmology. Other finds followed this discovery, but it took almost a century before sustained systematic archaeological work was begun.

The earliest major attempt to restore an archaeological site involved the Pyramid of the Sun at Teotihuacán not far from Mexico City. Work began in 1905. The overseer of the dig and restoration, an architect named Leopoldo Batres, has since received harsh criticism for his work, but in his day it was not possible to do much better. From 1917 to 1922, the Dirección de Antropologia, directed by Manuel Gamio, carried out major topographical surveys of the center of the ancient city, performed digs in buildings located on the eastern side of the Boulevard of the Dead and in the so-called Temple of Tláloc, and executed stratigraphic studies on various sites in the area, digging a tunnel all the way to the Pyramid of the Sun. In the end, crews managed to clear, probe, and rebuild all of the enormous temple known as the Ciudadela, or Citadel.

During the same period, Gamio organized the earliest stratigraphic excavations of Azcapotzalco, which led to the discovery of a number of cultural phases prior to those then known (viz., the Toltec and Aztec). Archaeologists began to speak in terms of a Formative or Archaic horizon, the exact chronology of which was uncertain but which would have been contemporary with the earliest farmers or ceramists in the region who created the many lovely statuettes found in a number of sites around the ancient Lake of Mexico.

Until that time, it was mistakenly believed that

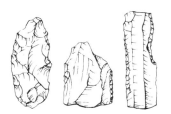

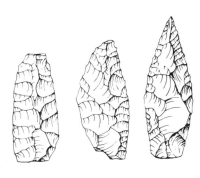

Stone tools found at Santa Isabel Iztapán, in association with mammoth bones.
(From L. Aveleyra, "The Primitive Hunters," in *Handbook of Middle America Indians,* vol. 1 [Austin: University of Texas Press, 1964])

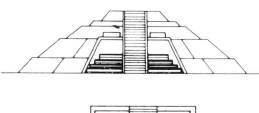

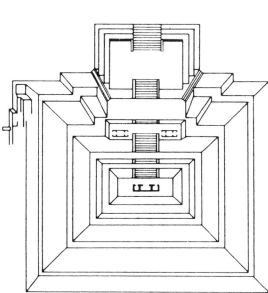

the ruins of Teotihuacán were the remains of the city of Tula, the ancient capital of the Toltec kingdom. Archaeological dating revealed that Teotihuacán had been built many centuries earlier than Tula. The true Toltec capital was discovered forty kilometers (25 mi.) further north in 1940. During the same period, the Pyramid of Cholula (not far from Puebla, to the southeast of Mexico City) was also explored. It was found that this pyramid originally stood taller than the Pyramid of the Sun and that it had been built during the same period in which the city of Teotihuacán was founded.

Archaeologists were also interested in when the circular pyramid of Cuicuilco (Mexico City) had

View of the stacked-structure circular base of Cuicuilco, a site on the southwestern shore of the Lake of Texcoco (Valley of Mexico), destroyed by lava flow in 200 B.C.E.

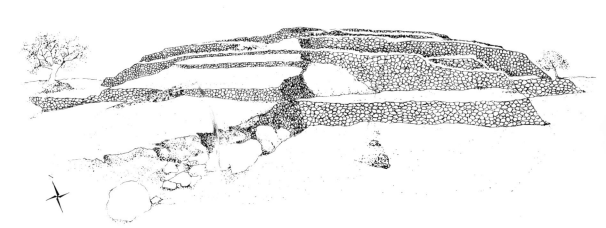

Top, right: *Elevation and plan of the Pyramid of the Moon of Teotihuacan (Valley of Mexico).*

been constructed. The lower platform of this pyramid was surrounded by a hardened block of lava. Investigations revealed that the lava was deposited following an eruption of the nearby volcano Xitle about two thousand years ago and that the pyramid had been built four centuries before that.

Around 1931, work began on the great ceremonial and funerary complex of Monte Albán, the capital of the Zapotec kingdom. The complex takes its name from a hill located not far from the city of Oaxaca. Here, too, an "archaic" building was discovered — El Templo de los Danzantes (the Temple of the Dancers) — which dates back before the time of the Zapotecs.

In 1946, the Dirección de Antropología was replaced by the Instituto Nacionál de Antropología y Historia. With the support of the Mexican government, this institute continued the established projects of excavation and restoration and also undertook a great many new projects. A National School of Anthropology and History was founded to train specialists, especially in fields involving the archaeology of monuments. A deparment of prehistory was also founded, specializing in the study of paleogeography and Preceramic cultures.

Studies of the "lithic phase" have been considerably advanced by the discovery of the two mammoths at Santa Isabel Izatpán (1954-1956) and intensive subsequent excavation of the Paleolithic encampment of Tlapacoya on the southeastern bank of the ancient lake of Mexico-Texcoco. Two North American teams of archaeologists have studied the area of Valsequillo (Puebla), an area rich in remains of Pleistocene fauna, and Sierra de Tamaulipas (1958) and Tehuacán (1964), which supported a series of cultures throughout the Holocene. Richard MacNeish, who led the expedition, found clear evidence of Preceramic agriculture in both regions.

It can safely be said that in 1964, with the inauguration of the National Museum of Anthropology in Mexico City, the cultural history of Mesoamerica had already been solidly established in its overall outlines, and its cultural development had been subdivided into three main phases: the Preclassical (formerly known as the Archaic), Classical, and Postclassical. At Teotihuacán, excavations went on without interruption. The Temple of Quetzalpapalotl (bird-butterfly) was unearthed, along with a great many of the city's ancient "palaces," and the Pyramid of the Moon was completely restored. The great artistic and cultural role played by this city in the first millennium C.E. was finally and definitively recognized.

The Citadel of Teotihuacan (Valley of Mexico), before and after the excavations done by Manuel Gamio.
(Gamio, 1922, plate V)

Top, left: *One of the* Danzantes *found during the archaeological excavations at the site of Monte Albán (Oaxaca, Mexico).*

The Piedra del Sol. *The stone disk (360 cm./142 in. in diameter) is in the collection of the National Museum Museum of Anthropology, Mexico City Bas-relief alternates in concentric circles, symbols, and glyphs of the Aztec ritual calendar. The face at the center is a combination of Tonatiuh, god of the sun, and Tlaltecuhtli, monster of the earth.*

(Photograph by A. Maffeis)

Facing page: The stone stairway, adorned with heads of feathered serpents, of the Temple of Quetzal-coatl in the Citadel. Miccaotli Phase, 150-250 C.E., *Teotihuacan, Valley of Mexico.*

(Photograph by A. Maffeis)

3 Prehistoric Forerunners: Preceramic Agriculture

WE HAVE ALREADY noted that agriculture — and, in particular, the cultivation of maize — lay at the foundation of Mesoamerican culture. We can benefit from MacNeish's studies of the cultivation of maize in the Tehuacán region during the El Riego phase, which lasted roughly from 7000 to 5200 B.C.E. The humans who lived in in this region during this period practiced seasonal nomadic migration. They formed groups that were larger than those of their predecessors, but their settlement pattern was quite different. The encampments dating from earlier periods were consistently quite large, while those of El Riego varied in size from large to small. MacNeish contends that this was the result of a seasonal alternation of "microgroups" and "macrogroups" hunting animals and scavenging for plants. They made use of pestles and *metates* (stone wheels used to grind grains), and they manufactured baskets, fiber mats, and cords for netting. The remains of a great many herbs as well as maguey, agave, and the fruit of cactaceous plants have been found in caves. Squash (probably of the *Cucurbita moschata* or *C. mixta* varieties) was probably in the earliest stages of domestication.

El Riego has also yielded the remains of burials with funerary furnishings such as baskets, netting, fiber textiles, and offerings of foodstuffs. The deceased were buried either lying down or hunched over in a funerary well. The remains of a cremated body have also been found. In another case, there is

evidence of the sacrifice of a child, probably in connection with cannibalistic rituals.

The Coxcatlán phase (5200-3400 B.C.E.) forms part of the so-called Tradition of the Desert, but with one significant difference: the diet of wild plants during this period was supplemented by a number of domesticated plants. Human settlements were much larger than in the previous phase, although the system of seasonal migration between larger and smaller centers continued. In one stratum, dating from around 5000 B.C.E., ears of primitive maize have been found — the oldest such remains in the world. The botanist P. Mangelsdorf has stated that the Coxcatlán variety of maize either grew wild or was in the earliest phases of domestication.

Remains of other plants, including avocados (aguacate), chili peppers, and squash (laghenaria) have also been found in this area and dating to this early period. Later, amaranth, tepary beans, zapotes (American medlars), and another variety of definitively domesticated squash appeared. The improvement of agricultural techniques shifted this culture increasingly toward a sedentary way of life. Vegetable remains typical of both spring and fall have been found in the same stratum, which would seem to point to a more sedentary lifestyle, although it falls short of establishing the existence of stable year-round dwellings. The *metates* acquired increasingly sophisticated shapes during this period, and they were joined by globe-shaped stone vases.

Sketch of a residential unit from the village civilization, in the Formative period, with fields of maize, tomb, well shaft for storage of provisions, and a subterranean oven.

(From Winter, 1989)

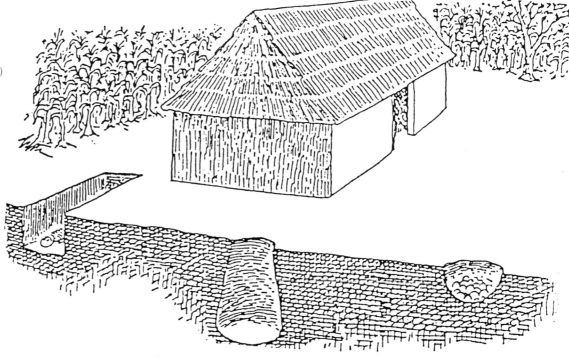

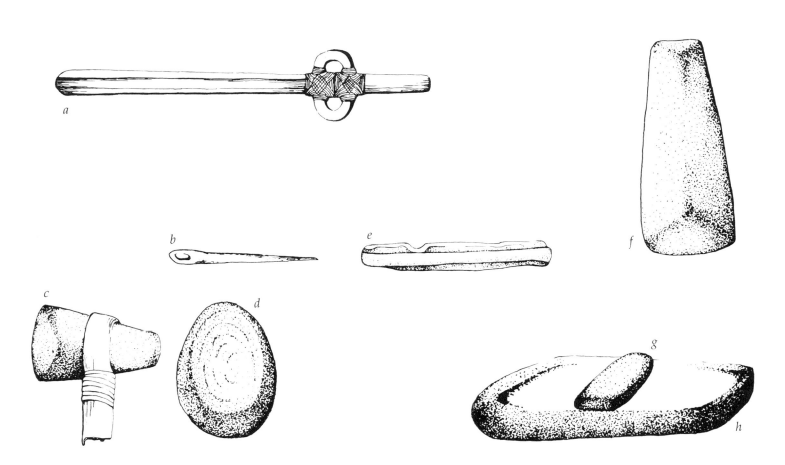

The subsequent period, known as Las Abejas (3400-3200 B.C.E.), was marked by an increase in the variety of both wild and domesticated plants in the diet. The first hybrid maize appeared, the result of cross-breeding maize with *teosinte,* a tall annual grass closely related to corn. Squash and amaranth were already common, but new strains were introduced, such as the *Cucurbita pepo* variety of squash, along with common beans *(Phaseolus vulgaris)* and cotton.

The communities grew in size and became stable. A new type of village made up of well-houses (i.e., partly buried dwellings) appeared; these houses were probably inhabited all year round. Small flakes of obsidian have been associated with these communities — the first evidences of this material, which eventually came to be intensely exploited in the Mesoamerican manufacturing technology. The use of globe-shaped stone vases continued, while the *metates* acquired an approximately rectangular shape, and the *manos* (pestles), which had previously been round, took on a flatter, wider shape.

The Las Abejas phase was followed by the Purrón phase (2300-1500 B.C.E.), characterized by villages associated with a clearly sedentary way of life, by the presence of a maize closer to the form we know, and by the appearance of ceramics. The latter development manifested itself in the form of ollas (pots) and plates that mimicked the prototypes in stone from the previous period, including the typical *tecomate* (a globe-shaped vase with a relatively small mouth, chiefly used as a receptacle for seeds and grains). With this phase (and another very similar phase in the Valley of Oaxaca), it is safe to say that the "Mesoamerican agricultural threshold" had been reached and that the Preclassical period had thus begun. Duing this period, all of the knowledge and lore of the previous cultures attained concrete form. The genetic improvement of food crops and the growing list of cultivated plants (not all of which were native to same area, a factor that suggests an active process of adaptation and interchange) laid the foundation for the beginning of what anthropologists call the Mesoamerican cultural tradition.

Tools from the Valley of Mexico, Later Preceramic period, 5000-2500 B.C.E.: (a) atlatl, *or spear throwing stick made of staghorn;* (b) *bone needle;* (c) *stone axe with wooden handle;* (d) *hammer-stone;* (e) *obsidian blade;* (f) *chisel- stone;* (g) mano, *or stone pestle;* (h) metate, *or grinding stone.* (From Piña Chan, 1955, and Weaver, 1981)

Top: *Plantation of persimmons in the Puebla area.* (Photograph by A. Maffeis)

Right: *Agave plants used to brew a beverage called* pulque. *The fibers were also used in making clothing.* (Photograph by A. Maffeis)

4 The Preclassical

Small terra-cotta heads found in 1958 in the landfill of a small leveled mound at La Venta, Tabasco. Olmec culture.

AT PUERTO MÁRQUEZ on the Pacific coast (circa 2400 B.C.E.) and inland at Purrón (2300 B.C.E.), protovillages from the Las Abejas phase adopted the ceramic technique for the fabrication of plates, dippers, and receptacles. In all likelihood, these communities derived techniques for the production of ceramics from the areas that are now Colombia and Ecudaor, where ceramics had already been common for several centuries. With the introduction of ceramics and the improvements in the cultivation of maize, a way of life began that has survived with few if any changes in the peaceful rural areas of Mexico to this day. Very little is known about the development of these communities, of the migrations they undertook, or the like. We do know where the earliest villages were located in the valley of Mexico from about 1800 B.C.E. on, especially at points surrounding the great central lake (El Arbolillo, Zacatenco). In what corresponds to the Lower Preclassical, a Neolithic way of life was the rule in these areas for more than a millennium, and there were no ceremonial centers. The ceramics, here as at Puebla (Ajalpán Phase, 1500-1900 B.C.E.), were monochrome and were distinguished by engraved geometric decorations and the appearance of new forms, including tripod vases. The similarity of this type of ceramic to that developed on the coast of the Gulf of Mexico and on the Pacific coast of Guatemala may well indicate that, in terms of pottery techniques, the cultures of Mesoamerica initially had a common tradition.

During the same period, female figurines made of clay similar to those found in Valdivia acquired a certain importance. As far as can be determined, the inhabitants of Tehuacán used these figurines in their religious practices, probably in connection with a fertility cult. The female figures, which were manufactured in great abundance at El Arbolillo and Zacatenco and shortly thereafter at Tlatilco and at other sites, had faces that were particularly well modeled, bodies that were were variously painted white, black, and red, and extremely elaborate hairstyles and headdresses that looked like turbans.

At the outset, the religion associated with these figurines involved belief in the existence of a life after death. The dead were buried along with vases and other objects, and small pieces of jade (considered symbolic of life in Mexico and elsewhere in the world, especially ancient China) were placed in their mouths. Most often bodies were buried beneath huts, according to Mesoamerican custom. In the rarer instances in which they were buried in cemeteries, the deceased would be wrapped in a mat with the knees raised to the chest and placed in a single grave dug in the sand, which was typically sealed with a stone slab.

After a certain period, the comparative social equality that had been the rule among these tribes broke down permanently. Agricultural production and associated wealth was concentrated in the hands of a very few, giving rise to a greatly stratified society. At the head of the community was a chief, usually a priest, who exercised preeminent economic, administrative, and religious power. In some cases, existing villages were transformed into ceremonial centers by the construction of religious buildings and monuments. More often, these ceremonial centers were erected in specific sites at a strategic distance from a group of villages, and the residents of the surrounding villages were required to perform religious service there. Further south, a powerful and prestigious priestly class that arose around 1200 B.C.E. pressed masses of people into service to build the first great Mesoamerican center of worship, San Lorenzo-Tenochtitlán, situated along the Atlantic side of the isthmus of Tehuantepéc.

The influence of Olmec culture is the overriding characteristic of the entire Middle Preclassical period. The evidence of its beginnings around 1000 B.C.E. includes the appearance in Mesoamerican sculpture of certain typologies, such as "baby faces" (actually faces with feline features). The best known site for these artifacts is a cemetery at Tlatilco, in the western sector of the Federal District of Mexico, where a rich array of statuettes constitutes the whole class of funerary accessories. Among these statuettes, the so-called *mujeres bonitas* ("beautiful women") stand out. There are also monstrous figures with large bulging eyes, two heads, and the like, the symbolism of which remains a mystery.

Among the new forms of pottery, two typically Andean typologies are particularly notable: a bottle with a globe-shaped body and a narrow vertical neck, and a pitcher with a pouring spout in the shape of a stirrup, which, as we have already noted, was previously present on the Ecuadorian coast (Machalilla Phase). More surprising forms include zoomorphic vases and a celebrated "acrobat" with his feet drawn around onto his head.

The first great pyramidal construction in the Olmec region (La Venta) was erected around 800 C.E.. Shortly afterward, a number of pyramids began appearing in central Mexico as well. Among these are the pyramid of Totimehuacán in the zone of Puebla-Talxcala and the circular pyramid of Cuicuilco. The latter, constructed around 4000 B.C.E., was originally distinguished by a base about 135 meters (445 ft.) in diameter and a height of 25 meters (85 ft.), with a stairway to the east and a broad stepped ramp to the west. Its shape is remarkable in the American context, where most such structures are either square or rectangular, with the sides oriented toward the cardinal points of the compass.

In the "sacred precinct" that surrounded this

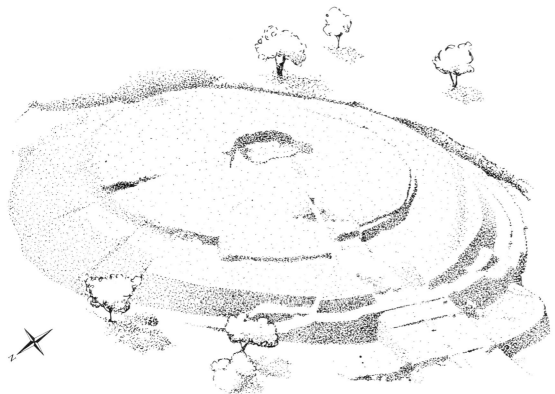

Design of the circular stone stacked-structure base of the pyramid of Cuicuilco, a site on the southwest shore of the Lake of Texcoco, destroyed by the lava flow from the volcano Xilte, in 200 B.C.E.

Following pages: *Cream-colored kaolin vase in the form of an acrobat, with the legs on the head; 22 centimeters (about 9 in.) high, from Tlatilco, Valley of Mexico.*

Terra-cotta figurine depicting a witch doctor with mask, helmet, and skirt. It is 8 centimeters (about 3 in.) high, and comes from Tlatilco, Valley of Mexico. Olmec culture.
(From R. Piña Chan, Olmechi, 1989)

Below: *Terra-cotta figurines with large bangs, slotted eyes, and Olmec mouth, from Tlatilco, Valley of Mexico. Olmec culture.*

construction, a number of interments have been found that are believed to be connected with ancient rites of initiation. This hypothesis seems to be confirmed by the existence of a small temple, set to one side of the pyramid, built with blocks of stone in the form of a small artificial grotto and decorated on the interior with curvilinear motifs in red. The Courtyard of the Dancers at Monte Albán (Oaxaca), which dates from around 700 B.C.E., constitutes another point of convergence with Olmec influences.

The symbology of the Dancers remains something of an enigma, not unlike that of the characters of the temple of Cerro Sechín in Peru. Are they prisoners being sacrificed, priests being mutilated or mutilating themselves, initiates in a trance state? What is the purpose of these depictions, and for whom were they intended? None of these questions has yet been answered in a satisfactory manner; we have nothing more than a series of hypotheses and the hope that additional archaeological investigation will provide answers. In any event, this first settlement at Monte Albán clearly established the site as a religious center devoted to the worship of various deities over a long period of time.

At a certain point in the Preclassic period there emerged a system of numbering and hieroglyphics that appears to be based on the calendar. This seems to be associated with the emergence of the classic Mesoamerican fifty-two-year cycle as well. This cycle was still in use during the time of the Aztecs, but it is different from that used by the Maya.

Under Olmec influence, it took only a few centuries to transform the central region from a simple society of villages to a growing social hierarchy. The change is evidenced by the presence of ceremonial platforms made of stone and earth and by interments distinguished by lavish funerary accessories. We are still uncertain about the precise means by which the changes took place, but we do know that in the final centuries preceding the Common Era, a full-fledged theocracy was being developed and consolidated. At a certain point, this theocracy manifested itself in a place located some fifty kilometers (30 mi.) to the northeast of what is now Mexico City. The small villages that had stood in the area were absorbed into what became the largest symbolic and ceremonial Mesoamerican complex, a city built in reverence to the deities who through their primordial sacrifice had given birth to the world and to humanity: Teotihuacán, the city of the gods.

5 The Culture of Teotihuacán: The History

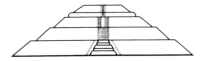

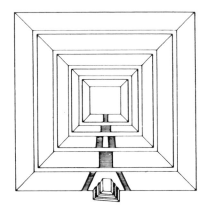

Plan and elevation of the Pyramid of the Sun, Teotihuacán, Valley of Mexico.

The Lake of Texcoco and the Valley of Teotihuacán. The great basin of water was formed by stagnant brackish waters and spring water.

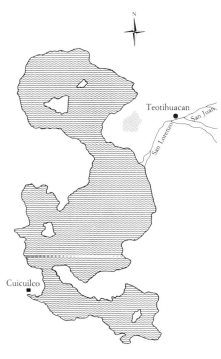

ABOUT 500 B.C.E., the valley of Teotihuacán was settled by a number of different groups of farmers who built their villages on the promontories and slopes that surrounded the valley to the north and the northwest. Among other centers, Maquizco, Cuanalán, and Patlachique were founded. As the population increased, a number of groups moved toward a flatter, more low-lying region crossed by the river San Juan, which until that time used only for hunting and agriculture. In the area called Oztoyahualco, a number of earthen platforms were built, along with a base for a pyramid made of mixed stone and clay. These constructions were soon covered by other buildings.

In ancient times, perhaps at the end of the Pleistocene, a stream had formed a broad tunnel that ran from east to west. This passageway served as the site of the earliest occult rites and initiatory rites in the area. Was it the presence of this sacred site that led to the construction of a platform above the tunnel at the end of the Local Preclassical period? What gave the local priesthood the prestige and power to found, without any preamble, an elite center that eventually outshone in size and magnificence all other sites in central Mexico? We do know that work began on the construction of the Pyramid of the Sun on this site around the beginning of the Common Era. This construction required sophisticated mathematical and architectural knowledge and a huge and extremely well-organized human work force. We also know that the construction of the pyramid took at least a century. Construction of Pyramid of the Sun ended during the middle of the Protoclassical period (ca. 0-300 C.E.), and construction of the Pyramid of the Moon began. By the end of the period, the great complex that stood nearby, known as the Citadel, was built. The whole complex was constructed close to the southern sector, which the Aztecs called the Boulevard of the Dead, believing the ruins of temples and palaces that lined both sides of the road to be tombs.

The beginning of the Classical period (around 300 C.E.) coincided with the beginning of the phase known as Teotihuacán III. Construction of the Citadel and of most of the buildings that lined both sides of the Boulevard of the Dead having been completed, the first true city of the Americas had arrived. The only significant remaining construction involved the addition of a number of residential buildings located outside of the boundaries of the main sector and the enlargement and renovation of some other buildings. Four centuries of intense and thoroughly planned architectural and artistic activity was followed by four more centuries devoted to the worship of the great terrestrial and celestial deities and to the establishment of stable commercial and religious ties with almost all of the regions of Mesoamerica.

During the second half of the seventh century C.E., this seemingly peaceful and secure way of life began to be disturbed. The city of Teotihuacán had grown to the point that it occupied most of the valley in which it had been founded; in the process it had become a major center of politics, commerce, religion, and craftsmanship. And yet its power as the capital of a great theocratic state was not linked to military might (as was the case with the Olmecs). No defensive fortifications were ever built around the city, and no one ever attempted to seize the city's wealth, perhaps because the value of that wealth was largely symbolic.

Despite this undisturbed state of peace, however, archaeological evidence points to a worsening quality of life in the later years. In the course of just a few decades, the city was almost entirely abandoned. There is evidence that fires were intentionally set in most of the temples and other buildings. Was this a result of a social revolution, attacks from other Mesoamerican city-states, or invasions from other "barbarian" peoples pressing in on the northern borders? Archaeologists now favor the third hypothesis. Michael Coe, for example, believes that intruders began to settle inside the ancient walls, in some cases burying their dead in the same places where the former inhabitants had buried theirs.

This "barbarian" occupation continued for three centuries following the destruction of the city, a period of time during which there developed a ceramic art form called Coyotlatelco, marked by the use of reds and greys. Although it never rivaled the handsome artifacts of Teotihuacán, it imitated the superior models at least in part. It is believed that refugees from the city gathered in the fairly small site of Atzcapotzalco, to the west of the great lake, and worked in vain to recapture the lost splendor of their ancient culture.

George Vaillant, on the other hand, has hypothesized that the extensive deforestation that had been necessary for the construction of Teotihuacán might have led to widespread erosion and thus to growing aridity in the region. This problem might have been exacerbated by the general decrease in rainfall experienced throughout Mexico during the Classical period, a phenomenon that would have had particularly serious effects in the Valley of Mexico. Vaillant maintains that the entire structure of the state of Teotihuacán disappeared during the agricultural disaster that occurred in the wake of the drought, leaving a vacuum that nomadic tribes from the northern border areas promptly filled, invading the civilized areas of Mexico.

Oswaldo Silva has argued that cultural evolution stalled in the city when the ruling classes proved unable to solve endemic problems and the peasants stopped supporting them as a result. The community slowly dissolved because there was no central

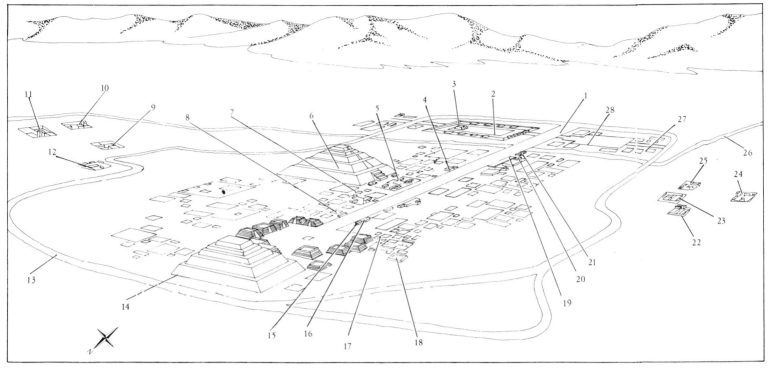

authority. Silva maintains that an intellectual vacuum and loss of prestige (which translated into a loss of power) on the part of the ruling elite was the leading cause for the abandonment of this and other classical cities. The absence of an accepted ruling class opened the door to the encroachment of other peoples that were culturally less developed; these invaders contributed to the definitive collapse of structures that had already been undermined. Mixing with the few survivors of the declining population, these invaders injected fresh new blood that made possible the transition to new and powerful phases of Mesoamerican civilization.

The fairly rapid decline of the city did not entail the disappearance of Teotihuacán culture, however. Various less distinguished incarnations survived in places such as Atzacapotzalco (which Vaillant associated with the Teotihuacán IV period), Cholula (where the tall pyramid, which was clearly an imitation of the Teotihuacán pyramids of the Sun and the Moon, remained in use for many years as an active religious center), and — with a few local

modifications — Xochicalco, on the southern fringes of central Mexico. The last-named city, situated atop a highland not far from Cuernavaca, inherited the cult of Quetzalcóatl and rendered it more powerful, a point to which we will return later.

Despite the striking archaeological remains of the Teotihuacán people, there is much about them that remains a mystery. Did the founders belong to a strictly local group, or — as a certain tradition would have it — did the Totonacs of the Veracruz area play a part? What language did they speak? Did they already speak Nahuátl, which was in use in the region during the Postclassical period? Their use of the symbols and the pictographic signs that they inherited from the Nahuátl does not necessarily mean that they spoke the same language, although it should not be entirely ruled out either. One thing that we know for certain is that Teotihuacán civilization was fully prehistoric (and premetallurgical) and that over the centuries that followed others spoke of it solely in legendary terms.

Elevation of a reconstruction of Teotihuacán: (1) *Boulevard of the Dead;* (2) *Citadel;* (3) *Temple of Quetzalcóatl;* (4) *Viking group;* (5) *Palace standing before the Pyramid of the Sun;* (6) *Pyramid of the Sun;* (7) *Palace of the Sun;* (8) *Mural of the Jaguar;* (9) *Xolalpan;* (10) *Tlamilolpa;* (12) *Tepantitla;* (13) *Modern road;* (14) *Pyramid of the Moon;* (15) *Temple of Agriculture;* (16) *Temple of Mythological Animals;* (17) *Palace of Quetzalpapalotl (Birdbutterfly) and, beneath it, the Palace of the Feathered Snails;* (18) *Courtyard of the Jaguars;* (19) *Square of the Western Complex of the Boulevard of the Dead;* (20) *Stacked buildings;* (21) *Northwestern Complex of the River San Juan;* (22) *Yayahuale;* (23) *Zacuala;* (24) *Atetelco;* (25) *Tetitla;* (26) *the San Juan River;* (27) *East-West Boulevard;* (28) *Marketplace.*

Following double-page spread: *Teotihuacán, Valley of Mexico, the Boulevard of the Dead seen from the Pyramid of the Moon. Left: The Pyramid of the Sun.*

(Photograph by A. Maffeis)

6 The Culture of Teotihuacán: The Art

Chalchiuhtlicue, goddess of water, found near the Pyramid of the Moon. Stone, 3.2 meters (10.5 ft.) tall.
(National Museum of Anthropology, Mexico City)

AT THE PEAK of its splendor, Teotihuacán was a full-fledged metropolis, with religious, civil, and residential sectors covering about twenty square kilometers (almost 8 sq. mi.) and with a population of at least eighty-five thousand. The core of the city was its ceremonial center. To the north stood the huge Pyramid of the Moon, at the foot of which there was a broad rectangular plaza punctuated by transverse walls fronting a series of courtyards that reached all the way to the Pyramid of the Sun and, further south, the Citadel. Not far from the Citadel, two long boulevards ran to the east and the west, giving the urban grid the distinctive cross-shaped scheme common to all of the ancient cities of America, Asia, and Europe.

Buildings were constructed by stacking layers of basic elements. The basic core was made of a conglomerate of mud, stones, and pebbles covered with an extremely fine layer of powdered stone. This was covered with a layer of particularly hard mortar, the surface of which was sanded very smooth, and this was given a finish coat of lime. The most important buildings adopted the *talud-tablero* structure. Layers of inclined modules *(talud)* were alternated with layers of rectangular modules *(tableros).* The *tableros* were often decorated on the upper and lower edges with paintings and bas-reliefs of various sorts. The finest example of this type of structure is the Pyramid of the Sun, one of the largest monuments in the Americas. With a virtually square plan (222 × 225 m., or about 728 × 738 ft.), the pyramid now stands 63 meters (207 ft.) tall, but probably once stood 75 meters (246 ft.) tall, because it was topped

by a temple, or adoratorium, that has since been destroyed. The access stairways leading to the top of the pyramid stood directly on each of the *talud.* The first structure possesses two stairways that mark off a second pyramidal structure that was added later. The entire structure stands atop a tall, broad platform, alongside which is located the so-called House of the Priests, made up of numerous courtyards, vestibules, and dwellings that are believed to have been used as priestly residences and as housing for the servants of the main temple.

The Pyramid of the Moon stands at the northern end of the great sacred road known as the Boulevard of the Dead. The smaller Pyramid of the Sun (42 m./138 ft. tall) has a structure made up of five platforms of various heights.

The vast complex of buildings known as the Citadel is made up of a square enclosure about 400 meters (1,300 ft.) on each side, flanked by various stepped buildings, the most noteworthy of which is the renowned Temple of Quetzalcóatl. The temple consists of six structures employing the typical *talud-tablero* scheme and features a considerable wealth of decoration, both sculpted and in relief. The decorations include depictions of feathered serpents portrayed amid seashells. Along the friezes, sculpted serpent's heads emerge from a sort of open flower, alternating with other serpent's heads that have been interpreted as depictions of the god Tlaloc.

Among the other building complexes are the Viking Group (named after the institution that sponsored the dig that uncovered it), which is located to the south of the Pyramid of the Sun; the so-called Stacked Buildings, which are situated on the opposite side of the Boulevard of the Dead; and the Temple of Agriculture, which located on the southern side of the huge plaza that stands before the Pyramid of the Moon. The Temple of Agriculture is made up of three stacked structures, added consecutively during three phases of construction. Also on this plaza, but to the west, stands one of the most interesting of the recently unearthed buildings, the Palace of Quetzalpapalotl (butterfly-bird), so named because its rectangular columns bear engravings of a creature with the characteristics of both a bird and a butterfly.

Apart from the pyramids and the major residential complexes, most of the buildings found in the area of Teotihuacán were the residences of the lords of the city — the same situation as that found in Xolalpan, Tetila, Tepantitla, Zacuala, and Atetelco. The structure of these buildings follows that of Xolalpan, a complex with an overall rectangular shape containing no fewer than forty-five residences and seven courtyards surrounding a central courtyard set below ground level with a small altar at its center. There were no windows, but some of the

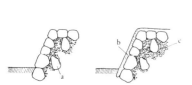
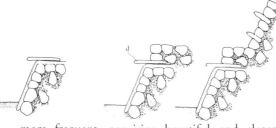
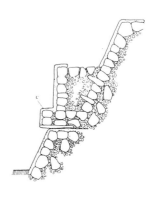
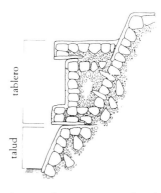

courtyards had small secondary courtyards though which light and air could enter. When necessary, it was possible to draw rain water from cisterns and reservoirs set below ground level. All of the residential buildings that we have found were one story in height and had flat roofs supported by small beams.

The artistic refinement that this civilization attained is partially indicated by the magnificent frescoes they left behind on the walls of their buildings, for the most part depictions of various deities. The walls of the White Courtyard of the Palace of Atetelco, for example, contain rows of jaguars and coyotes painted in various colors. The Palace of Tepantitla contains a great multicolored fresco depicting the Paradise of the Rain King (Tlalocan). A depiction of Tlaloc himself dominates the fresco; drops of water fall from his hands, while beneath a few small human figures play, sing, and laugh, and butterflies and flowering trees further enliven the scene. The whole amounts to an heavenly paradise where all those who have died in some way from water (drowning, floods, etc.) go when they die.

The painting of Teotihuacán reached its greatest height during the third phase, whereas sculpture (which on the whole was far less significant than the painting) reached its height in the second phase. The aesthetics and forms of Teotihuacán art generally accord with the severe style of its architecture: they are both marked by a striving toward spareness and hieratic solemnity, in some cases reminiscent of the art of Tiahuanaco in the Andean area.

The highest expression of the culture of Teotihuacán is the large anthropomorphic monolith erected in the plaza standing before the Pyramid of the Moon, built in honor of the Goddess of Water, Chalchiuhtlicue.

We have made valuable finds in the area of pottery production, such as the many female figurines continuing the ancestral Preclassic tradition, which are characterized by an outstandingly stylized realism, especially in the faces, hair and jewelry. The bodies are sometimes naked, sometimes dressed with skirts and shirts.

During the Teotihuacán II period, fictile technique reached a high level of perfection. The best example of this is a type of highly refined pottery called point cloisonnè, multi-colored and lacquered, which was used in ceremonies; another style of pottery similar to this is called "delicate orange" because of its extra fine mixture. However, Teotihuacán pottery reached its highest peak during the Classical period, when the shapes of ceremonial vases become varied and elegant. Many are jars or earthenware pots with the edges curved outward and one or two lips for pouring. But most numerous are exquisite cylindrical vases covered with onyx with cone-shaped lids and three legs. This fine pottery with an orange-colored base becomes more and

more frequent, acquiring beautiful and elegant shapes. Point cloisonnè pottery is found in a visually stunning array of pastel tones: pink, turquoise, gray, white, and golden yellow ochre.

Finally, it is important to mention the many specimens which are created by applying the champlevé, or scraping method. The figurines present familiar shapes, but with a more sophisticated technique and a higher level of realism. Typical of this period are the "articulated dolls."

Many of these objects, which show a high level of specialization, have been found in near and distant Mesoamerican places, where they arrived through trade or were made by Teotihuacán industries located in strategic sites. In distant Guatemala, the Classical phase of Kaminaljuyu is characterized by the Teotihuacán style of architecture. By the same token, "embassies" of other cities existed in Teotihuacán itself, identified by the unique style of the pottery found.

Phases in the construction of a talud-tablero: (a) *landfill made with volcanic stone;* (b) *mortar and plaster;* (c) *pebbles bound with mud;* (d) *andesite slab to support the* tablero; (e) *cornice of the* tablero.

Facing page, bottom: *Water Deity with two assistants, upper panel of the mural of Tlalocan at Tepantitla. Copied in the collections of the National Museum of Anthropology, Mexico City.*

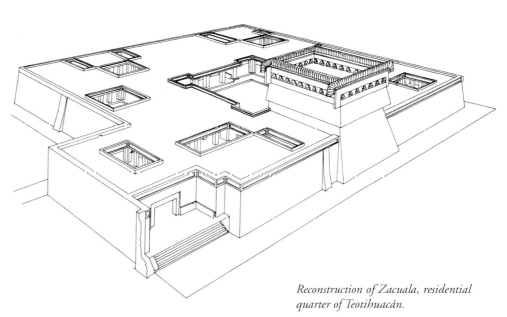

Reconstruction of Zacuala, residential quarter of Teotihuacán.

Mask from the Museum of the Templo Mayor, Mexico City, made of hard stone sanded and polished with applications of obsidian to imitate pupils; 20 centimeters (about 8 in.) tall. (Photograph by A. Siliotti)

Facing page: *Teotihuacán, Valley of Mexico, the Pyramid of the Moon, southern face, and the Plaza of the Moon, seen from the top of the Pyramid of the Sun.*
(Photograph by A. Maffeis)

7 The Culture of Teotihuacán: Politics and Religion

Priest in the murals of Casa Barrios, at the Teopancalco site to the south of Teotihuacán.

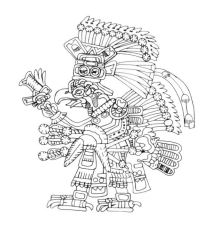

Eagle warrior, with darts and dart-launcher in hand.

Terra-cotta figurines indicating how the Teotihuacán aristocracy dressed. Many show an intentional cranial deformation.
(National Museum of Anthropology, Mexico City)

Jaguar warrior in the murals of Zacuala, Teotihuacán.

IN GENERAL, the culture of Teotihuacán led to the first political and cultural unification of the region of central Mexico and to an authentic level of civilization. Without that unifying culture, there could never have been the successive developments of the Toltec kingdom and the Aztec empire. The unification was based chiefly in mythical and religious concepts. The prestige of the priestly class of Teotihuacán endured through centuries, to the point that later generations remembered those priests as being giants. Later legends held that it was specifically at Teotihuacán that the gods gathered in order to begin a new era after a dark period. Under the direction of Nanahuatzin, "the purulent one" (who first hurled himself into a fire and then transformed himself into the Sun), the gods sacrificed to create humanity and the world as it is now. The name Teotihuacán means both "city of the gods" and "city where men are transformed into deities." According to native tradition, the Boulevard of the Dead was lined with the tombs of ancient kings and lords whose spirits had risen to the divine realm.

These beliefs are associated with the importance of initiation rites in the culture of Teotihuacán and the preceding Olmec culture. Furthermore, these mythological traditions were precursors — and concise versions — of the more familiar myths and ceremonies of subsequent Mesoamerican cultures.

Teotihuacán produced the earliest versions of such figures as Huehueteotl, the old god of fire; Xipe-Tótec, "our lord, the flayed one," who was meant to symbolize the annual rebirth of plant life; the cosmic deities (the great Sun and Moon pyramids celebrate these deities and were probably used as astronomical observatories, much like the ziggurat of ancient Mesopotamia); Tláloc, the god of the rains (or, more precisely, of the water that renders fertile); and Quetzalcóatl, the "bird-serpent."

Quetzalcóatl was a symbol of an essential and eternal duality — life and death. The serpent from the earth, where life has its origin, attempts to reach the heavens in the form of a bird. The morning star, Venus, gathers the light of the Sun that dies each evening and announces its imminent rebirth. We do not know whether Teotihuacán culture identified Quetzalcóatl as a historical or mythical personage, as was the case from the Toltec period on, when the most important king identified himself with this deity, but archaeological investigation has turned up a ceramic fragment bearing a figure with a short beard joined to the symbol of the feathered serpent, suggesting that the people of Teotihuacán may well have known Quetzalcóatl as the civilizing god about whom later traditions speak. If, as many believe, the Citadel served as a royal palace, it could surely have been the center of an official cult

centered on Quetzalcóatl as the tutelary god of the city and the protector of the city's rulers.

In any event, Teotihuacán's deities eventually formed part of the Toltec pantheon and, consequently, the Aztec pantheon as well. The philosophy of life associated with worship of these gods survived until the Spanish conquest, contributing to the creation of the distinctive Mexican unity. The spirit of Teotihuacán is still evident in the following piece of indigenous poetry, transcribed by Fra Bernardino da Sahagún a few years after the conquest:

And this they call Teotihuacán,
because it is where they bury the lords.
And it is said: "Even if we shall die,
we shall not die
because we shall continue to live
until our rebirth.
And we shall be happy."
And the deceased shall hear these words:
"Reawaken when the sun
shall cause the dawn to begin,
and the flame-colored worms
and the colorful birds and the butterflies
shall take flight."
Because the old ones say that "he who dies
shall be a god."

The reference is to Quetzalpapalotl, symbolically depicted as a bird-butterfly (a worm transformed). A temple-palace at the foot of the Pyramid of the Moon is also dedicated to this god.

The conflagration that consumed Teotihuacán was the first of a series of catastrophes that afflicted all of the cultural groups of the Classical period between the eighth and ninth centuries C.E. Specialists believe that invasions or popular uprisings were no more than secondary causes of the cultural decline, the primary cause being a sort of internal decadence, a "spiritual breakdown" of the ruling theocratic elite, both here and at Monte Albán and among the classic Mayans of the Guatemalan Petén.

But the flame was not entirely extinguished. Cities such as Cholula and Xochicalco, where Quetzalcóatl was worshiped, sustained and transformed the culture during the transition to the Postclassical period, the initial phase of which was constituted by the Toltec kingdom. Tula, the capital of the Toltec kingdom from 967 to 1168, fell to a group of "barbarian" warriors from the north (Chichimecs). At the same time, however, a major group of Toltecs moved to the Yucatan, where they founded the city of Chichén-Itzá.

Various lords continued to struggle for power in the Valley of Mexico. In the fourteenth century, a group said to come from a mythical place called Aztlán founded the city of Tenochtitlán on an island in the Lake of Mexico. This group was the Mexica, better known as the Aztecs. The Aztecs

considered themselves the rightful heirs to the Toltecs, and therefore to Teotihuacán. Their religion included in a more limited form an element that had long been a part of previous cultures — namely, human sacrifice. They sought to feed the deities (especially the Sun) with the precious ambrosia of human blood in order to repay them for the sacrifice that had produced the human race in the first place. The "wars of flowers" were apparently organized to provide an unlimited supply of new prisoners to sacrifice. This led to the ascendancy of the warrior sun god Huitzilopochtli over the peaceful god Quetzalcóatl. But part of the feathered serpent's wisdom survived and merged — in more or less syncretic forms — with Spanish Christianity.

The god Huehuteotl. Stone, height 36 centimeters (14 in.).
(National Museum of Anthropology, Mexico City)

Following double-page spread:
Reconstruction of Teotihuacán at the time of the construction of the Pyramid of the Moon and the palace of Quetzalpapalotl.

Drawing of the oval panel of the "Palazzo," Palenque, Chiapas.
(Drawing by M. G. Robertson, from *The Sculpture of Palenque,* vol. 2 [Princeton: Princeton University Press], fig. 91)

PART IV

The Olmecs and the Maya

Playing pelota at Chichén-Itzá, in northern Yucatan. This is the largest pelota court in the Americas. Mayan culture.

Monument 1, La Venta Museum, Villahermosa, Tabasco. Olmec culture. Colossal head, in basalt, 241 centimeters (95 in.) in height.

Temple of the Cross in Palenque, Chiapas. Mayan culture.

● Mayan sites
◆ Olmec Sites
■ Sites influenced by the Olmecs

Dzibichaltún

Chichén-Itzá

Uxmal

Sayil Labná

Kabáh

Yucatán

Area of development of gulf coast Olmec culture

Mexico City

Laguna de Términos

Tres Zapotes

Grijalva

La Venta

San Lorenzo Teñochtitlán

Usumacinta

Uaxactún

Palenque

Tikál

Pedras Negras

ISTHMUS OF TEHUANTEPEC

Yaxchilan

Bonampak

Monte Alban Oaxaca

Quiriguá

Copán

Izapa

Influences of Ecuadorian-Colombian traditions

Kaminaljuyu

Amatitlan

Monument 56, La Venta Museum, Villahermosa, Tabasco. Olmec culture. Sculpture, in basalt, 241 centimeters (96 in.) in height, depicting a monkey.

103

1 Geography and Natural Regions

The forest in its natural form, little changed over the centuries, is now faced with the danger of being transformed into a wasteland unless current destructive processes are replaced with conservative forms of restoration. Over the course of the centuries that separate the Mayan civilization from ours, the regenerative power of the forest has been so great that unused roads and paths regularly disappeared without a trace in a few years, and foliage would completely conceal temples, pyramids, and even entire cities as little as fifteen or twenty meters from an observer.

THE TERRITORY of Mesoamerica is traditionally divided into two sectors: central Mexico and the Mayan area. The sectors are divided by by a loosely defined line that runs from the extreme southernmost point of the Gulf of Campeche in a south-by-southeasterly direction to the Pacific Ocean near the modern-day border between Mexico and Guatemala.

Archaeological sites that have uncovered evidence of the ancient Mayan culture are scattered through the Central American countries of Mexico (Tabasco, Chiapas, and the Yucatan peninsula), Guatemala, and Belize and in a strip running north to south along the western section of Honduras and El Salvador.

Altogether, the Mayan area can be split into three main geographical areas: the south, comprising the mountainous tropical zone of the highlands of Chiapas and Guatemala; a central area (the most important region in terms of the culture of the Mayan Classic period), which includes the hill country and wooded plains of Chiapas and the Petén of Guatemala; and the north, more or less corresponding to the Yucatan peninsula. The two most important rivers in the area begin in the mountains of the south and run down to the central area. The Usumacinta River runs to the northwest, and the Motagua runs to the northeast. A third river, the Grijalva, runs across the states of Chiapas and Tabasco and empties into the Gulf of Mexico. The Yucatan peninsula is a limestone plain devoid of rivers. The ancient inhabitants of this area got their water from *cenotes* (sinkholes in the limestone with pools of water at the bottom) or built cisterns to capture rainwater.

The climate of the central area is generally hot and rainy, producing a rich vegetation. The heavy rainfall feeds many rivers, streams, marshes, and swamps that manage to persist during the dry season. The few mountains that exist in this area are no higher than six hundred meters (2,000 ft.) above sea level.

In the higher elevations of the southern area, the climate is temperate, and the forests are chiefly made up of pine trees and mahogany. The tallest mountains in this region are in western Guatemala and include the Alto de Cuchumatanes (3,900 m./12,800 ft.) and the volcanoes of Tacana (4,000 m./13,100 ft.) and Tajumulco (4,200 m./13,800 ft.). To the northwest, in Belize, the Mayan Mountains are no taller than 1,000 meters (about 3,300 ft. above sea level).

Agricultural methods vary considerably, depending on the climate. The natives of the lowlands typically used the slash-and-burn technique to prepare fields for the planting of corn. In the highlands, on the other hand, the fields were cultivated for as much as ten years consecutively, making possible far greater concentrations of population and the development of numerous villages.

The Mayan archaeological area corresponds, in general terms, to the region of *mayances* languages — that is to say, those groups belonging to the Mayan linguistic family (unlike the inhabitants of Teotihuacán, the Maya had a language of their own). Scholars of linguistics believe that numerous groups native to northeastern Guatemala have spoken this language since the local Preclassic period. Today only about two million people still speak the Mayan language, 1.4 million of which live in Guatemala. Only a small group, the Lacandón Indians in the central part of the Usumacinta River basin, has managed to avoid the influence

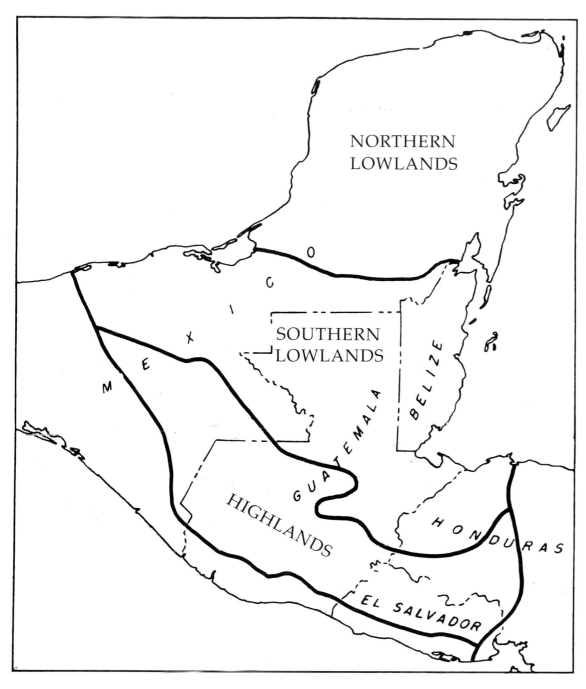

NORTHERN
LOWLANDS

SOUTHERN
LOWLANDS

O
C
I
X
E
M

B
E
L
I
Z
E

G
U
A
T
E
M
A
L
A

HIGHLANDS

H
O
N
D
U
R
A
S

EL SALVADOR

Map of the different areas in which the Mayan civilization developed. To the south, the highlands witnessed the birth of Mayan civilization in the Preclassical period. The lowlands of the south were the site of the great and small kingdoms of the Classical period. The lowlands of the north were the site of the development and decline of the Postclassical Mayans, who were later subjugated by the Spanish.

of other modern languages. Michael Coe contends that the Olmecs were predecessors of the Maya and spoke a language that was related to Mayan. He contends that the region of Olmec settlements around the Gulf of Mexico and extending inland in a southeasterly direction overlaps with an area inhabited by "proto-Maya." Other scholars have argued that the Olmecs spoke a language belonging to the Mixe-Zoquean linguistic family.

Whatever the connections between the Maya and the Olmecs, however, the distinctions between the two cultures are sharp, especially if we associate Mayan culture with the inhabitants of those cities in the geographic zones described above that produced a hieroglyphic system of writing, a calendar, and a classical architectural style beginning in the third century C.E. We cannot speak with any certainty about what preceded this era. Among other things, we cannot conclude from the fact that some version of the Mayan language was spoken in much of the region that the Maya themselves existed prior to the third century C.E. On the other hand, the development of Mayan culture is inconceivable without the foundations of Olmec culture, and so we would do well to consider something of the history and development of that culture by way of introduction.

Top: *Temples of Palenque, Chiapas. Mayan Classical period. At the center, almost swallowed by the forest, stands the Temple of the Leafy Cross, on the left is the Temple of the Cross, and on the right is the Temple of the Sun.*
(Photograph by A. Maffeis)

Facing page, bottom left: *Typical vegetation of Tabasco, the state in which the ceremonial center of La Venta once stood, one of the most important of Olmec settlements.*
Facing page, right: *The slash-and-burn system of farming.*
(R. Piña Chan)

Left: *The river runs toward the sea, the natural setting for Olmec settlement near the Gulf of Mexico.*

2 Olmec Culture: The History of the Discoveries

Partial plan of the Ceremonial Center of La Venta, Tabasco.
(from Drucker, 1952, and Piña Chan, 1982)

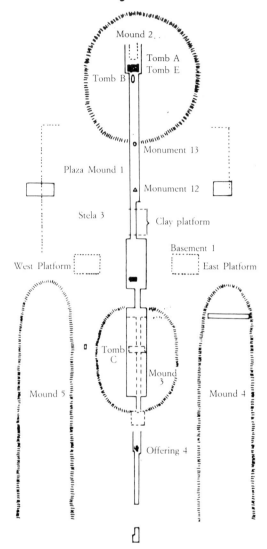

Mound 2
Tomb A
Tomb E
Tomb B
Monument 13
Plaza Mound 1
Monument 12
Stela 3
Clay platform
Basement 1
West Platform
East Platform
Tomb C
Mound 3
Mound 5
Mound 4
Offering 4

Altar 4, La Venta Museum, Villahermosa, Tabasco. Basalt monolith, 160 centimeters (63 in.) in height and 319 centimeters (126 in.) in width.

OLMEC CULTURE is one of the most important cultures to have been discovered during the twentieth century. Because of its considerable antiquity and influence, many view it as the "mother culture" of Mesoamerican civilization. Although the distinctive statuettes and axes made by the Olmecs were well known during the nineteenth century (Baron Alexander von Humboldt brought one of the axes back to Berlin when he returned from his celebrated "voyage in the equinoctial zones"), it was not until 1925 that the first exploration of the "Olmec core region" was organized, in Los Tuxtlas and surrounding areas in the state of Veracruz. During that exploration, Frans Blom and O. La Fargue discovered the ruins of La Venta and attributed them to the Maya.

At the time of the Spanish conquest, the Aztecs called the wild lowlands of the Gulf *Olman,* meaning the "land of rubber," and later the archaeologists coined the term *Olmec* to refer to the ancient natives of this area. George Vaillant was the first to speak of an "Olmec complex," characterized by depictions of felines or human beings with feline features. In the course of his excavations in the Valley of Mexico, while exploring the most ancient sites, he found objects made of jade and ceramics marked by this style, and he thought that they might have been of southeastern origin.

Another North American archaeologist, Matthew Stirling, began to explore Tres Zapotes and La Venta in 1938. There he discovered, along with stelae and altars, a number of the famous giant "Olmec heads," which stood more than two

Offering 4 found in Complex A of the Ceremonial Center of La Venta, Tabasco. Examples of similar votive statuettes have been found in the various ceremonial centers of the Olmecs. This offering consists of fifteen figurines made of jade and serpentine, one figurine made of granite, and six axes, arranged in a semicircle, suggesting a counsel of chiefs or a rite of initiation.
(From R. Piña Chan, Olmechi [1989])

meters (7 ft.) tall and weighed nearly twenty metric tons each. A scholarly consensus was reached in 1942 during during a roundtable discussion in Mexico, and the identification of Olmec culture was made official, although a number of doubts still existed concerning its specific chronology. In 1945-1946 Stirling and Drucker discovered the complex of San Lorenzo-Tenochtitlán, at a distance of about one hundred kilometers (62 mi.) from La Venta. Excavations were completed between 1964 and 1967 by Michael Coe of Yale University. In the meantime, other sites were explored by a number of Mexican archaeologists, among them A. Medellín Zenil and Román Piña Chan. Michael Coe used radiocarbon dating to establish that the site of San Lorenzo (1250 B.C.E.) represented the most ancient phase of this culture; he also reached the curious conclusion that the monumental Olmec heads had been sculpted in the suffocating jungles of the Gulf at a time when Mesoamerican peasants were still shaping crude figurines.

San Lorenzo was first occupied around 1500 B.C.E., and by around 1250 B.C.E. the first ceremonial platforms and drainage canals had been built on an artificial terracing structure. For the next three hundred years, a priestly elite of unknown origin directed the natives of the area in the work of building the site and transporting and sculpting the stone blocks used in the altars, the stelae, and the earliest giant heads. Olmec artists also created statuettes and a noteworthy array of tools and utensils from a great variety of materials, including serpentine, flint, and obsidian, most of which came from nearby sites.

Plan of San Lorenzo, Veracruz, with the ceremonial center in the middle.
(From Coe, 1967, and Piña Chan, 1982)

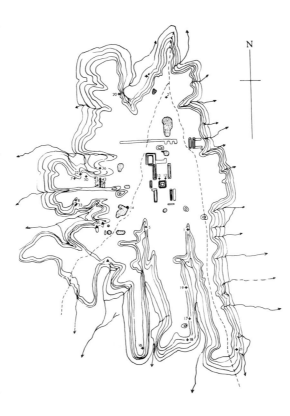

Monument 17 from San Lorenzo,
Veracruz: a colossal stone head carved
from basalt standing 167 centimeters
(66 in.) in height.
 (From R. Piña Chan, Olmechi [1989])

Facing page: Monument 1 from San
Lorenzo, Veracruz: a head known as
El Rey, carved from basalt standing
285 centimeters (112 in.) in height.
 (From R. Piña Chan, Olmechi [1989])

3 Olmec Culture: The Art

Hollow "babyface" figure made of whitish terra-cotta, 21 centimeters (8 in.) in height.

(From the Leolf collection)

Basalt sculpture, about 90 centimeters (35 in.) in height, originally from Iztapa, Chiapas

WITH SAN LORENZO, the first great Meso-american artistic style was born, based in turn on the first great religious cult, characterized by the symbol of the feline — or, more specifically, the jaguar. Despite this, it is still not possible to speak of an urban culture here, because the permanent core population at San Lorenzo was no greater twenty-five hundred. It increased only sporadically and temporarily as groups drifted in from nearby satellite towns such as Tenochtitlán and Potrero Nuevo.

The cult of the feline, which also developed in other ancient cultures of the Americas, has its highest expression in the "werejaguar" (an English name given to establish an analogy with the northern European legend of the werewolf). Shamanistic practices were aimed at bringing about a "complex of feline transformation," bringing humans into contact with a deity in the shape of a jaguar and gradually causing them to identify themselves with that deity. A number of Olmec statues portray this transformation. The cult of the feline also sustained a legend that in the remote past a woman was made pregnant by a jaguar and generated a race of humans distinguished to a greater or lesser degree by feline features. Several statues uncovered in Olmec territory portray this mythical act of copulation; statues of figures from the resulting race of jaguar-men generally depict them as sexless and pudgy or baby-faced.

Around 900 B.C.E. San Lorenzo was partially abandoned, and many of its monuments were intentionally mutilated for reasons that have not yet been determined. The power that had been concentrated there passed to La Venta, situated in what is now the Mexican state of Tabasco, near the northern boundary of the Mayan area. A number of magnificent ruins and artistic artifacts have survived from this great center.

The site of La Venta is situated on an "island" in the midst of a swamp, some thirty kilometers (20 mi.) inland from the coast. This island is about five kilometers (3 mi.) long and one kilometer wide, with its main axis running from north to south. A number of ceremonial complexes were built along this axis, mostly large rectangular earthen structures. Among them is the oldest pyramid ever discovered in Mesoamerica, a great truncated cone some thirty-five meters (115 ft.) tall, erected on a rectangular platform made entirely of pounded earth. There are no ramps or stairways giving access, although there probably was a small temple atop the pyramid.

The ceremonies at La Venta were probably conducted inside the two rectangular plazas surrounded by basalt columns set on adobe bases. The complex was closed off to the north by a stepped earthen hillock. Many of the walls and floors were covered by stucco, colored red, yellow, and purple. Both in this complex and in another one located further to the south (the Stirling Group, which consists of a plaza and a number of rectangular hillocks, or mounds), there were a great number of monuments made of basalt, including stelae, altars, and sculptures of all sorts, including examples of the colossal Olmec heads, the symbolic meaning of which is still much debated.

Various archaeological digs at La Venta have uncovered evidence of ritual offerings, statuettes, and other objects at a number of places. Of particular beauty are three mosaic floors made of green serpentine depicting a huge stylized jaguar mask. Currently, all of the site's stone monuments and one of the mosaics are in the Natural and Archaeological Park of La Venta at Villahermosa.

Another important find was that of a tomb in one of the hillocks. The funerary chamber, made out of basalt columns, contained the remains of two young men, probably dignitaries or priests, intended for sacrifice. Their bodies were covered with heavy red mantles (the color red was a universal symbol of life), and they were surrounded by a great quantity of figures and objects made of jade.

Silva has pointed out that political power at both San Lorenzo and La Venta extended beyond the ceremonial center proper. La Venta, for example, could not house more than 250 people at a time, and yet far more would have been needed to construct the pyramid alone. According to one estimate, the territory ruled by La Venta covered approximately nine hundred square kilometers (350 sq. mi.). Assuming a population density of 20 inhabitants per square kilometer (about 52 people per sq. mi.), the total population would have been about 18,000 individuals. La Venta's social structure involved three distinct levels: a peasant class, a middle class made up of craftspeople, and an elite priestly and political class at the top.

La Venta flourished at the time of the greatest expansion of Olmec influence to the south and southwest (ca. 900-400 B.C.E.). The main driving force behind this expansion appears to have been a search for jade, which had a special value for the Olmecs in the production of statuettes and ornaments. A number of surviving ceremonial centers and interesting bas relief rock carvings bear witness to the existence of full-fledged colonies allied with the core region. Important examples of such colonies are Chacaltzingo in central Mexico and Tonala-Tzutzuculi, Xoc, and Pijijiapan in the center and the south of Chiapas, on the boundaries of the classic Mayan region.

It seems clear that active commerce took place between the core Olmec region and the Balsas River basin, central Mexico, and areas located to the south and southeast, along the isthmus of Tehuantepéc and the coastal strip known as Soconusco, all the way down to Guatemala and El Salvador, where both pure Olmec and "Olmecoid" monuments have been found. Some isolated Olmec monuments have also been found well within the Mayan region, which proves that there was some sort of contact — commercial if no other sort — between the Maya and the Olmecs.

La Venta began to decline in the fifth century B.C.E. much as San Lorenzo had four centuries earlier (albeit more gradually) and for similar reasons. Evidence indicates that its monuments were violently defaced before the center was finally abandoned.

There is clear evidence of a final flourishing of this culture further west, at Tres Zapotes and in other sites in the state of Veracruz. A monument built in this region shows clear connections between the Olmecs and the Maya. The C stela bears the signs of a numerical system in general use among the Maya. Dots or circles indicate individual units, and lines or dashes indicate quantities of five. Evidence seems to suggest (1) that at a relatively advanced stage in the development of their culture, the Olmecs invented a calendar as well as a numerical system, (2) that this calendar was quickly and widely adopted by other peoples of southern Mesoamerica, and (3) that the Maya later adopted and perfected this calendar, adding it to a second calendrical system (the so-called Long Cycle, which was linked to the solar year).

Between the first century B.C.E., during which the last Olmec groups disappeared or were assimilated by other groups, and the third century C.E., when the construction of the chief Mayan cities began, there were a number of phases about which we know very little, the most important of which is the Izapa phase, centered in the extreme southeastern portion of modern-day Chiapas. The sites that exemplify this phase constitute examples — both in terms of chronology and typology — of a transition between Olmec and Maya. Given the absence of any Olmec ceremonial centers in Mayan territory, however, we have to characterize the ancient Olmec culture as only an indirect precursor of Mayan civilization.

Still, there is a great body of compelling evidence that points close links between the Olmec and Maya — the similarity between the settings in which the two cultures developed; the probable relationship of the Olmec tongue to the Mayan linguistic family; the ceremonial centers, or "open cities," that the Maya transformed into theocratic city-states; the symbolism of the jaguar, which was upheld (in an attenuated form) among the Maya; and the way in which jade and other artistic and cultural forms were used. All these things would seem to indicate that, despite the formal and stylistic distinctions and the great chronological gap between the Olmecs and the Maya, the prehistoric Olmecs did constitute the "mother" culture to the classic Maya and the other principal cultures of central Mexico.

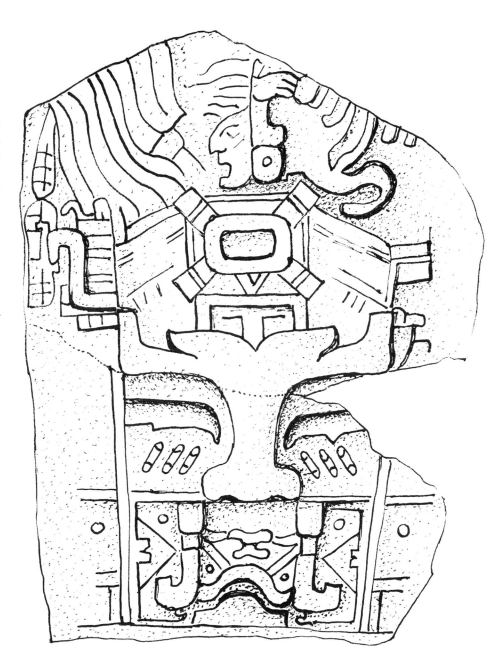

Relief carved in basalt from the front section of Stela C, Tres Zapotes, Veracruz, 160 centimeters (63 in.) in height.

Following pages: *Monument 19, a stela 95 centimeters (37 in.) in height, featuring the figures of a rattlesnake, the deity of the Celestial Water, and a priest linked to that cult.*

Right side of Altar 5, showing two priests holding children, probably for sacrifice. (Photograph by A. Maffeis)

4 Mayan Civilization: The History of the Discoveries

BEFORE MOVING ON to a consideration of the outstanding features of six spectacular centuries (300-900 C.E.) of American and indeed universal culture, we should take some note of the history of the discovery of various Mayan sites.

Aside from a number of discoveries that took place during colonial times, the pioneering explorer of the Mayan ruins was the "French count," as he is so often described (apparently, he was actually an Austrian baron), Jean Fréderic Waldeck, who visited this zone between 1820 and 1830. At Palenque, the

Self-portrait by A. P. Maudslay in the studio he set up inside the Palace of Nuns at Chichén-Itzá.

"Pyramid of the Count" commemorates his two-year stay. In 1834 he began to explore the city of Uxmál, and in Paris in 1838 he published an illustrated book presenting the results of his research. The true discoverers of Mayan culture, however, were the American John Lloyd Stephens and the Englishman George Catherwood, who was an excellent draftsman among other things. In 1841 Stephens and Catherwood published a book together entitled *Incidents of Travel in Central America, Chiapas and Yucatán,* and two years later they produced a book devoted solely to Yucatán. In their books they described all that they had been able to see in the Mayan territories then accessible. These two works and the drawings by Catherwood made a great impression on public opinion and the scientific world, but conditions were not yet ripe for the organization of detailed explorations and archaeological excavations adequate to free the ruins from centuries of encroaching vegetation.

During the second half of the century, new expeditions were organized by Desiré Charnay of France (1885), Alfred Maudslay of England (1899), and Teobert Maler of Austria. Maler produced some of the finest photographic records of the era, and his work was published by the Peabody Museum at Harvard University. The same institution sent a great many scientific expeditions to Mayan territory that opened paths into the dense tropical jungle and brought to light many relics of this civilization.

The Carnegie Institute of Washington funded additional subsequent research. Sylvanus Morley and, later on, J. Eric Thompson worked on Carnegie expeditions to decipher the Mayan system of calendar numbering and the hieroglyphic writing. One unquestionably spectacular and decisive moment in the archaeological investigation of Maya culture took place with the discovery of the Tomb of Palenque by Alberto Ruz Lhuillier in 1952.

The science of ethnohistory — the study of traditions and historical documents that in this case date mostly from around the time of the Spanish conquest — have also greatly expanded our understanding of this fascinating and complex culture. Among the most important works to have been subjected to ethnohistorical analysis are the *Popol Vuh* (a creation story of the Quiché people of Gatemala) and the *Chilam Balam.* Also important is the work of Abbot E. Brasseur de Bourbourg, who published the *Popol Vuh* in French in 1867 and who was the first to make use of the chronicles of the Bishop Diego de Landa concerning the customs and traditions of Yucatán. Regrettably, as in the case of Teotihuacán, no oral traditions from the Mayan Classic period itself have survived.

The north facade of the Temple of Inscriptions of Palenque, Chiapas.
(Photograph by Teobert Maler)

Rendition of the bas-relief on the sarcophagus cover in the mortuary crypt of the Temple of Inscriptions of Palenque. The bas-relief appears to depict King Pacal as he descends to the underworld.
(Drawing by M. G. Robertson, in M. G. Robertson's *The Sculpture of Palenque*, vol. 2, fig. 73 [Princeton: Princeton University Press])

Bottom left: *Uxmal, Arch of the Governor's Palace, pencil drawing in two colors, by Catherwood.*

Following pages: *Stela H, at Copán, in a drawing by Catherwood.*

Temple of Inscriptions, at Palenque. Overall view, as seen from the "Palace." (Photograph by A. Maffeis)

5 Mayan Civilization: The History

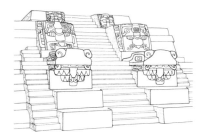

Drawing of the stairway that leads to the entrance of the temple, Pyramid E-VII South, Uaxactún, Guatemala. The masks, modeled in stucco on either side of the staircase, are an example of the initial Mayan style.

Drawing of a fresco at Bonampak, Chiapas. A nude prisoner begs for mercy from victorious lords. Other prisoners, their hands bloodied, sit on lower steps alongside a prone body, the foot of which lies near the hacked-off head of a prisoner who has been sacrificed.

(Drawing from H. J. Henderson, *The World of the Ancient Maya* [London, 1981])

IN HIS BOOK *The Ancient Maya* (1947), S. G. Morley makes a distinction between a Mayan "Old Kingdom" and "New Kingdom," perhaps taking his inspiration from the way in which the history of ancient Egypt is divided. But since there never was a unified Mayan kingdom or empire comparable to that of Egypt, it would probably be more helpful to work in terms of the standard Mesoamerican nomenclature of Preclassic, Classic (= Morley's "Old Kingdom"), and Postclassic (= Morley's "New Kingdom") periods.

Archaeologists have uncovered evidence of two principal ceramic phases within the Preclassic period. The first takes its name from Kaminaljuyu in the Guatemalan highlands but also includes artifacts found at Arévalo (1100 B.C.E.), Las Charcas (1000-600 B.C.E.), and other sites. The second series, associated with sites in the central area dating from 1200 to 800 B.C.E., is known as the Mamon phase. The earliest known expressions of Mayan art and architecture made their appearance in the subsequent Chicanel horizon; among these are the E-VII-sub pyramid at Uaxactún, where huge mascarons with the features of a jaguar, set along the sides of the stairway that leads to the upper platform, reveal a clear Olmec tradition.

Other sites, explored only recently, date from the Late Preclassic period and reveal more typically Mayan features. Such is the case in Cuello (in

northern Belize) and Komchén (in northern Yucatan), for example, where buildings have been dated to around 400 B.C.E. The most noteworthy example, however, is that of El Mirador in northern Guatemala, where construction began in 150 B.C.E. on the north side of the plaza of one of the largest pyramids known — El Tigre, which stands fifty-five meters (180 ft.) tall and features three temples on the upper section. On the southern side of the same plaza, the building known as Structure 34 was decorated with stucco mascarons representing jaguar heads measuring over two meters (more than 6 ft.) in size. Just two kilometers away from El Tigre, the Danta site features two large stepped terraces set alongside a hillock and a tall temple set on the upper area. In these and other sites, remains have been found of wooden enclosures not unlike the stone enclosures built during the Classic era. Despite the fact that these sites do not coincide with the best known cities of the Classic and Postclassic periods (except for Uaxactún and Tikál), and setting aside the antecedents from Olmec and Izapa culture, these finds indicate that the Mayan civilization developed *in loco*.

The Classic period is customarily said to have begun in the year 292 C.E. — the date engraved on the C Stela of Tikál. A number of cities developed during this period in the lowlands of the central zone. Tzacol ceramics are characteristic of the first phase of the Classic period (300-630 C.E.); the second phase, during which the great flowering of Mayan art took place, lasted another 250 years but ended rather suddenly between 880 and 925 C.E. The Classic period was characterized by a number of architectural and cultural elements, including the false vault, the measurement of time through two cross-referenced calendar cycles, a hieroglyphic system of writing, and considerable mathematical and astronomical learning. There are clear signs that contact with Teotihuacán culture began around 400 C.E. (probably through Kaminaljuyu, which became a sort of colony of Teotihuacán). At the same time, a number of well-known Mayan cities were founded, such as Dzibichaltún in Yucatan and Comalcalco in Tabasco, not far from the Olmec center of La Venta, which had been abandoned by this point.

This Classic period was followed by a brief period (925-975 C.E.) that J. Eric Thompson refers to as "transitional" and that was characterized by a fairly low level of culture.

One of the more important developments at the end of the Classic period was the cultural and artistic complex known as Puuc, in the hill country that bears the same name, located to the west of the Yucatan peninsula between the modern-day cities of Mérida and Campeche. It is believed that a number of Mayan groups from the south moved to

settle in this relatively arid zone and produced number of cities. Their settlements feature a striking new architectural style that incorporates cultural features from a variety of eras along with some features of their previous home. The architectural features of Puuc have also been found outside this region, at Chichén-Itzá.

The most handsome and best known city in the Puuc style is Uxmál, which has been almost entirely rebuilt. Other urban complexes in the area include Kabáh, Sayil, Xlapák, and Labná. The most distinctive features of Puuc architecture include a contrast between vertical walls with smooth facades and richly ornamented friezes (in some cases, small distinctive columns are used), the use of stone mosaic, and, in general, abstract ornamental compositions associated with religious concepts. Both the constructions and the figures have regular and harmonious dimensions and demonstrate a skillful blend of realistic depiction and religious symbolism, offering a fair indication of the spiritual conception of the universe held by the artists who created them. The architecture is perfectly integrated with the sculpture and painting (very little of the colors used in the paintings has survived, but it appears to have had only symbolic value). The anthropomorphic sculpture is quite realistic while at the same time abounding in allusions to religious practice.

The Puuc group survived for several centuries in various areas of the Yucatan peninsula, and in particular at Chichén-Itzá, but during the Ancient Postclassic period (975-1200 C.E.), Mayan-Toltec culture also developed in this region. Following the migration of Toltec groups from central Mexico, many features of this culture became associated with the existing Mayan culture, producing architectural forms and ornamental motifs that resemble prototypes in the city of Tula. The Mayan pantheon was enriched by Toltec deities such as Quetzalcóatl (whose Mayan name was Kukulkán, meaning "feathered serpent"). On this point, archaeological findings echo legend — specifically, the story that the Toltec king Quetzalcóatl, having been banished from Tula, moved his court to Chichén-Itzá at the end of the tenth century C.E. There are various architectural and ornamental features common to both cultures, including columns in the shape of feathered serpents, friezes depicting running jaguars or warriors, pilasters, Atlases in the form of dwarfs, and *chac-mol* (characters seated in a distinctive position).

Following this period of rebirth, Mayan culture entered a long slow period of decline, eventually entering what has been called the period of "Mexican Absorption," which corresponds to the Late Postclassic period (1200-1540 C.E.). During this period Mayan families established alliances with families of Nahua origin that created internal divisions and gave rise to wars that accelerated the process of cultural deterioration. When the first Spanish explorers reached the area in 1524, few traces remained of the ancient and splendid Mayan civilization. Some priests consulted with peasants and helped to preserve a record of the ancient traditions, transcribing them in pictographic codices and books, but most of these were ruthlessly destroyed by Spanish priests consumed with religious zeal. Three Mayan codices survived intact, however, and are now in European collections. In addition, some traces of the ancient Mayan language are believed to have survived in the speech of Lacandón Indians, residents of the central area of the Usumacinta River basin who are believed to be modern descendants of the once-great culture.

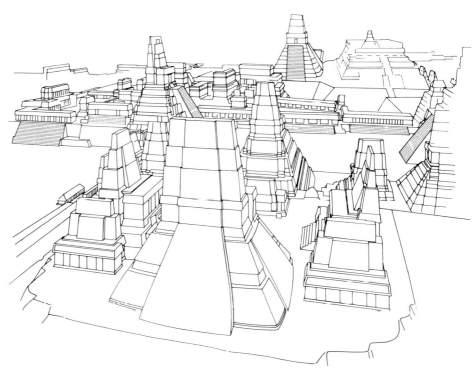

Reconstruction of the center of Tikal, Guatemala.
(Drawing from W. R. Coe, *Tikal: A Handbook of the Maya Ruins* [Philadelphia: University of Pennsylvania, 1967])

Drawing of the façade of the Castillo, Chichén-Itzá, Yucatan. The tableros that adorn the monument diminish in size as one moves upward, giving the structure a particularly upward-soaring appearance.
(Drawing by A. Arroyo G., based on the work of M. A. Fernandez, in Marquina 1951)

Chichén-Itzá, Yucatan. From atop the Castillo, one can see the Temple of Warriors, and — on the right — the Courtyard of the Thousand Columns.
(Photograph by A. Contri)

Palace of Nuns, Uxmal, Yucatan
(Photograph by G. Ganora)

6 Mayan Civilization: The Art

Drawing of Stela 4, Machaquilá, Guatemala. The figure is holding a "mannequin scepter" (God K), symbol of power (late Classical period).
(Drawing by Ian Graham)

THE MAYAN ECONOMIC and political system was based on city-states centered in temples that were governed by a priestly elite acting in the name of the deities. The *halac huinic* ("true man") was considered to be the supreme authority; his power was, with a very few exceptions, hereditary. This political system was broadly accepted by the lower classes (craftspeople, merchants, and peasants), and even the ruling classes of the various cities seem to have respected one another: there are no records of wars among them. Nonetheless, there were warriors who were equipped with wooden and stone weapons; here, as at Teotihuacán, metallurgy was unknown.

Society was extremely stratified, and yet there was no slavery. Trade was organized by the state and conducted with cities that constituted important centers of exchange. There were manufacturing centers for the production of a number of types of goods and centers of distribution for trade by land, river, and sea. Raw materials and finished and partly finished materials were exported, in some cases to considerably distant markets.

Mesoamericans living in the cultures of the Classic period probably felt that they were part of a cosmic order, experiencing a harmonious universal rhythm that was represented and elucidated by the priests. They may not have felt, therefore, that the burden of this rule was in any way unjust.

All the same, at a certain juncture, this society fell into a sudden decline. There is as yet no firm consensus concerning the factors that initiated the decline, but various scholars have argued that shifts in the climate, loss of fertility of the fields due to excessive agricultural exploitation, and an intellectual and moral decline on the part of the ruling class led to a state of rebellion (a sort of "civil disobedience") among the peasants and craftspeople

and eventually caused them to abandon the ceremonial centers of the region. The latest recorded date, found on a stela at Uaxactún, corresponds to the year 889 C.E.

Now that we have considered the principal aspects of Mayan society, let us examine more specifically Mayan art, beginning with architecture.

Mayan cities featured central cores made up of one or more plazas, religious and administrative buildings, and marketplaces surrounded by the main public buildings. The outskirts of the cities were made up of various neighborhoods, largely built out of perishable materials. The most important cities of the "Old Kingdom" were Copán and Quiriguá in the Motagua River basin; Uaxactún and Tikál (the latter being the most magnificent and also probably the oldest) in the Guatemalan region of Petén; and Yaxchilán, Piedras Negras, Bonampak, and Palenque in the Usumacinta River basin. The basic building material was high-quality limestone, which is quite abundant in the ground of this region.

The two most important Mayan building types were temples and palaces. The temples, rectangular in plan, were built atop truncated pyramids. One reached them by climbing a main ramp that typically rose along the front of the temple and secondary ramps in form of long stairways. A temple interior usually comprised one or more halls, and one of these halls constituted the sanctuary proper. The interior of one of the pyramids of Palenque contained a tomb that featured a stone sarcophagus closed with a richly carved slab and held the remains of a priest-king adorned with a great quantity of jade. The sarcophagus was set in a room the walls of which were covered with bas-reliefs depicting scenes that are presumed to be mythological in nature.

Panoramic view from the north of Palenque, Chiapas.
A. *Palace.*
B. *Temple of the Inscriptions.*
C. *Temple of the Bas-Relief.*
D. *Temple of the Cross.*
E. *Temple of the Sun.*
F. *Temple of the Cerro.*
G. *Mouth of the aqueduct.*
H. *Controls of the aqueduct.*
I. *Far upper reach of the aqueduct.*
(Drawing by W. H. Homes, in Marquina 1951)

Drawing of Stela 31, Tikal, Guatemala. This monument was built around 445 C.E. *in order to mark the end of the first* katun *of the government of Stormy Skies. The costumes are substantially Mayan but are clearly inspired by the style of Teotihuacán. The figures on the sides of the stela are styled as warriors of Teotihuacán: they hold throwing-sticks, and their shields — on the right — are adorned with the face of Tlaloc, the Central American god of rain. The head looking down is that of Sneering Face, predecessor of the god of Stormy Skies. The glyph of his name appears as part of his hairstyle. The head of the deity that emerges from that glyph, and a number of elements of the hairstyle of the heads hanging at his belt, may constitute linguistic signs. The hieroglyphic text tells of the rise to power of Sneering Face and Stormy Skies, emphasizing their genealogical ties.*

(Adapted from Maya Sculpture from the Southern Lowlands, the Highlands and the Pacific Piedmont [Berkeley, 1972])

It is believed that the palaces were the residences of the priests and their closest collaborators. These palaces were built on low platforms and typically contained a great many rectangular enclosures and doorways to admit light. Light also entered through small windows of various shapes. Inside, the constructions were covered by "false vaults." Facing walls were constructed to be thicker at the top than the bottom — so thick near the peak as almost to touch each other. Flat stone slabs were then placed over the small remaining gap between the tops of the walls, thereby closing off the "vault."

A similar architectural feature was also used in prehistoric cultures of western Asia and the Mediterranean, though the Maya were the only ones to make use of it in a systematic manner. They appear to have invented it on their own. Another distinctive feature of Mayan architecture was the battlements, or "giant comb," found on the roof of many ceremonial buildings.

The larger architectural structures were typically adorned with great numbers of bas-reliefs made with carved stone and with modeled stucco, which was often painted in many colors. Architects must thus have worked closely with sculptors and plasterers. Even to the modern eye, the ornamentation, the proportions of the figures, and the interplay of shadow and light appear to have been carefully coordinated, and the delicate lines still arouse admiration. The Mayan culture went beyond pure and simple decoration, endowing ornaments with a complex religious symbolism.

In the applied arts as well, the Maya attained remarkable levels of virtuosity. Archaeologists have uncovered extremely well made ceramics, both engraved and painted, vases with and without covers, cylindrical receptacles with particularly refined walls, and three-legged vases with covers (the shape is typical of Teotihuacán, but the decorations are distinctively Mayan). Polychrome painting was done on an orange or neutral-colored slip. The decorative motifs were zoomorphic or anthropomorphic, often depicting scenes of everyday life or monstrous figures, along with glyphs and abstract elements. The site at Jaina, an island located off the western coast of Yucatan, has yielded many small anthropomorphic sculptures of richly dressed individuals.

In addition to the forms of sculpture already mentioned, Mayan culture produced bas-reliefs of human and divine figures, half-bust statues, commemorative stelae, stucco and mosaic masks, and bas-reliefs on wooden boards that were used to decorate the innermost walls of a number of temple enclosures.

Following pages: *Masculine mask from Jaina, Campeche. High Classical period.*

Feminine figure from Jaina, Campeche. High classical period.
(Photography by A. Maffeis)

Chichén-Itzá, north Yucatan. From atop the Temple of Warriors, one can see the chac-mool *located at the top of the stairway of the temple. In the broad plaza, on the left, is the Castillo; the eastern side of the pelota court is visible in the distance.*
(Photography by A. Contri)

7 Mayan Civilization: The Religion and Writing

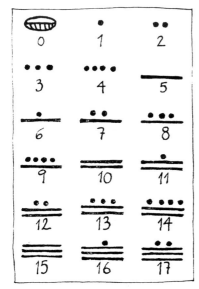

The Mayan numerical system.

Signs of the months in inscriptions.
(Drawing based on the work of
C. P. Bodwitch, in S. G. Morley's
*Introduction to the Study of the Maya
Hieroglyphs* [Dover, N.Y., 1975])

A COMBINATION of ethno-historical data and archaeological finds from the Postclassic period have given scholars a fair basis for the reconstruction of the Mayan religion. Given the powerful Toltec influence, however, it is not easy to apply these data to the religion of the Classic period. It is, in any case, necessary to distinguish between folk religion, which still survives in legends and folklore, from the "official" religion of the upper classes, which is attested by the art and architecture. Almost certainly Mayan culture followed other ancient high cultures of the Americas and Asia in supporting both a ceremonial cult and and an esoteric cult. The ceremonial cult would have had a specific symbology associated with festivals, the calendar, and agricultural cycles; the esoteric cult would have been associated with initiatory practices of the high priests and the *halac huinic* of each. The theocratic systems of ancient Mesoamerica and other cultures, such as that of ancient Sumer, involved the organization and direction of social life by a priestly elite, which acted on behalf of and by inspiration from the deities. Ancient Mayan religion appears to have been fundamentally astral in nature, though this would not necessarily have excluded a naturalistic and earthly counterpart. In any case, astronomy and the calculation of time were important features of the religion.

The ancient Mayan religion also placed significant stress on cosmogony, which is mentioned even in late documents such as the *Popol Vuh,* which speaks of four epochs prior to our own, each of which had ended with a great cataclysm ordered by the gods to eliminate imperfections that had arisen during the previous epoch. Only after discarding races of imperfect creatures (who were transformed into monkeys, etc.) did the gods create the human race as we know it and assign it the task of invoking and serving the deities (a task that included "feeding" them with various sacrifices, including human sacrifices). Still, there was a sense that even this present creation stood under the threat of eradication, and so, at the beginning of each new year and at the end of every calendar cycle, special liturgies were employed to preclude an apocalypse. Nonetheless, the specter of imminent catastrophe became an obsession for the Maya and led them to expand the practice of human sacrifice that they had taken over from the Toltecs.

Drawing on ethnohistorical research, Henri Lehmann has provided a brief description of other aspects of the Mayan vision of the cosmos. They envisioned the universe as being constructed of thirteen heavens and nine subterranean worlds. The heavens, stacked one above the other, were called *Oxlahuntikú,* and our earth was the bottom-most of these. The subterranean worlds were called *Bolontikú,* and the bottom-most of these belonged to the

Lord of Death. The Mayan pantheon was variously populated: every world had its own god, as did every natural phenomenon, every day *(kin),* every twenty-day month *(uinal),* and every twenty-year period *(katún),* at the end of which a commemorative stela was erected. Both the Maya and the Aztec adopted a form of dualism. All benevolent deities (e.g., the gods of rain, thunder, and lightning) had corresponding malevolent deities (e.g., the gods of drought, storms, war, etc.).

The creator of the world was Hunab. It was believed that his son Itzamna, lord of the heavens, lord of night and day, had given the Maya the gift of writing, codices, and perhaps the calendar, and so Hunab was invoked in the ceremonies of the new year aimed at preventing calamities and disasters. The cult of Hunab was often associated with the cult of Kinch Ahau, the god of the sun. Chaak, the god of the rain, played a very important role, particularly in the Yucatan. Chaak was typically represented, both in codices and in sculpture, as having a very large nose and was often associated with Kukulkán, the god of the wind. The god of maize, or, more generally, of agriculture, was generally depicted as a young man who — on certain occasions — held up an ear of maize. We do not know his name, but he was often identified with the letter *E.* The god of death was called Ah Puch and was depicted as having a skull stripped of flesh and wearing a great number of rattles. Not surprisingly, he was associated with the god of war, Ek Chuab.

All these deities were worshiped in a strict, intricate, and inflexible manner: religious ceremonies were preceded by fasts or other extreme forms of abstinence. Sacrifices of various sorts played an overwhelming role in Mayan religion. During the "Old Kingdom" period, sacrifices mostly involved offerings of food, animals, or precious objects. During the "New Kingdom" period, there was a greater emphasis on blood sacrifices, including human blood. It was customary for worshipers to draw their own blood by using flint knives or fish bones to pierce either their earlobes or their tongues. It was not until later, in the Yucatan (in what were known as "jaguar" or "warrior" temples), that depictions began to appear of human sacrifices — the sort of sacrifices that astonished the Spanish conquistadores and gave rise to legends of these peoples' cruelty.

The astral aspects of Mayan religion were connected with accurate methods of timekeeping. The Maya eventually perfected the calendar system that had already been used by the Olmecs and other Late Preclassic groups. They established a sacred year *(tzolkin)* made up of thirteen months of twenty days each and another year that corresponded to the solar year *(haab)* and was made up of eighteen months of twenty days each; the five additional

days needed to fill out the total of of 365 were considered ill-fated. Each month had a corresponding glyph. The two calendars intermeshed like cogwheels of different size. It took 73 rotations of the religious calendar and 52 rotations of the civil calendar — a total of 18,980 days — for a given date to recur. At the end of each 52-year period, known as a "Mayan century," great festivities were held. Historical chronology (used to indicate the dates on which cities and temples were founded and to commemorate such events as the turn of Mayan centuries and the coronations and deaths of kings) used what is known as the Long Count, a complex system of calculation. The Long Count began in the year 3113 B.C.E.

The astronomer priests knew that a solar year was not exactly 365 days in length, and they developed a system of correction to maintain accuracy in chronology over longer periods of time. This system led to the development of the Short Count in the Postclassic period. Scholars have succeeded in determining the correspondence of Mayan dates with our modern calendar by working backward from a known date shortly after the Spanish conquest.

The Mayan hieroglyphic system has proved more difficult to decipher than the calendar. Scholars have managed to assign meanings to only 250 of 700 known glyphs.

Taken as a whole, the "lost cities" of the classic Maya form a unique culture, giving evidence of a change from a theocratic system to a system with a political and military foundation. Oddly, while the dominant city, probably Tikál, attained a population of forty thousand, the cities of Petén and the surrounding areas lost their inhabitants. The power fell into the hands of the Puuc, and later into the the hands of the group centered in Chichén-Itzá. Mayan culture existed as such only during the time in which it became an organic part of the larger American civilization. Given the intellectual heights it reached and its splendid, complexly symbolic art, it has rightly been described as the "most perfect pearl" among all the great cultural movements that developed in the Americas. Its crisis and decline, its metamorphoses and resurrections constitute a story that still captivates scholars. We have secured an adequate explanations of the "hows" of the Maya, but we still cannot explain the "whys," and we may never succeed in fully understanding the mentality that underlay this great culture.

Detail of a drawing of the frieze along the bench at the pelota court at Chichén-Itzá, in northern Yucatan. At the center is the pelota, or ball, with a symbol of death. The players, richly dressed as ritual demands, advance toward the ball. The player in front of the group on the right is kneeling and headless, and from his neck spurts blood transformed into leaves and flowers. The player who leads the group on the left holds a knife in his right hand, and in his left hand dangles the head of the beheaded player.

(Drawing by M. A. Fernandez, in I. Marquina, 1951)

a   *b*   *c*   *d*   *e*   *f*

g   *h*   *i*   *j*   *k*   *l*

Phonetically based glyphs.
(Drawing based on the work of C. P. Bodwitch, in S. G. Morley's *Introduction to the Study of the Maya Hieroglyphs* [Dover, N.Y., 1975])
Following double-page spread:
Reconstruction of th ceremonial center of Chichén-Itzá.

*Zoomorphic motifs on one of the stele which remain as
testimony to the Chavín culture.*

PART V

The First Andean Empire: Chavín

Bottle with zoomorphic decoration from the region of Tembladera, Cajamarca, Peru. Chavín culture.

Bas-relief from the Middle Temple of Garagay, Lima, Peru. It depicts a monstrous head with feline fangs. Chavín culture.

Anthropomorphic bottle from the region of Tembladera, Cajamarca, Peru. Chavín culture.

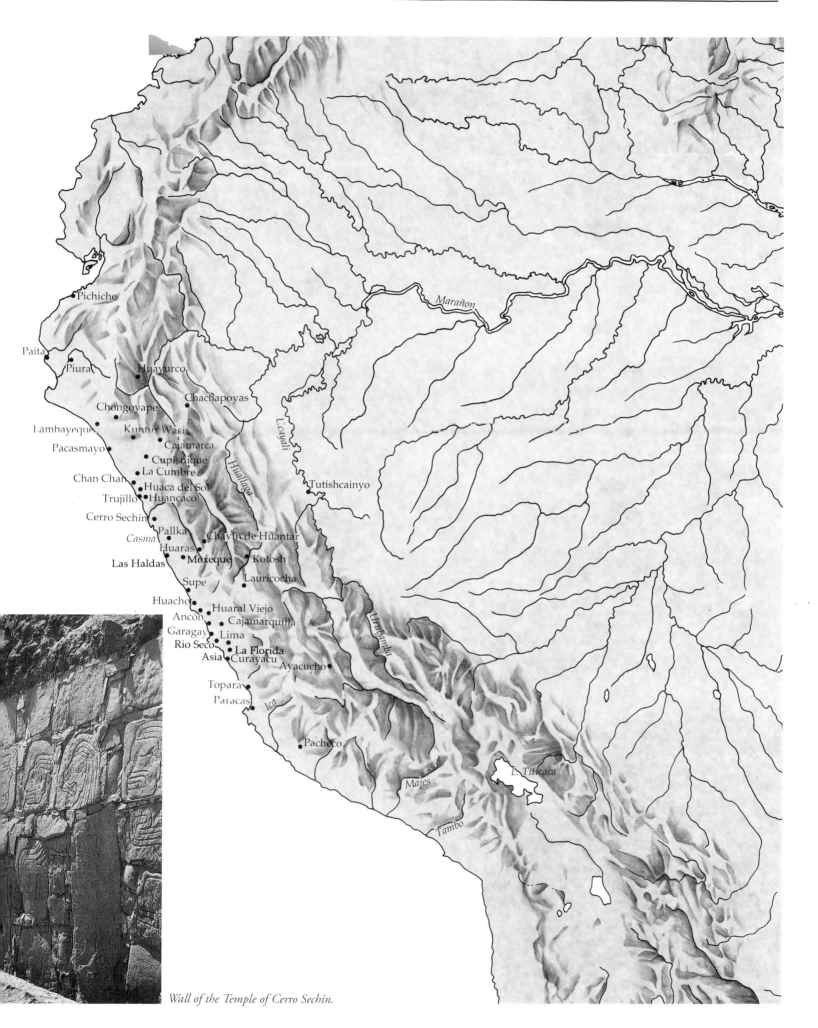

Pichiche

Paita

Piura • *Huayurco*

Chachapoyas

Chongoyape

Lambayeque • *Kuntur Wasi*

Pacasmayo • *Cajamarca*

Cupisnique

Chan Chan • *La Cumbre*

Huaca del Sol

Trujillo • *Huancaco*

Cerro Sechín

Pallka

Casma • *Huaras*

Las Haldas • *Moxeque* • *Kotosh*

Supe

Lauricocha

Huacho

Huaral Viejo

Ancón

Cajamarquilla

Garagay • *Lima*

Río Seco • **La Florida**

Asia • *Curayacu*

Ayacucho

Topara

Paracas

Ica

Pacheco

Marañon

Ucayali

Huallaga

Tutishcainyo

Chavín de Huántar

Urubamba

Majes

L. Titicaca

Tambo

Wall of the Temple of Cerro Sechín.

135

1 Geography and Natural Regions

ANDEAN CULTURE is the second great social and artistic formation of pre-Columbian America. It developed along the Cordillera of the Andes, covering a territory that ranges from southern Colombia and Ecuador all the way to northwestern Argentina and northern Chile. Debate continues as to whether all of Colombia belongs in this territory, including the part outside of the Amazonian forest, which — along with Ecuador — constitutes the Northern Andean Area, or whether it more appropriately belongs to the "intermediate" or Central American area. There are also doubts concerning the southern boundaries of the Andean territory. Western Argentina and central Chile are generally included in the Southern Andean Area, although the cultures of this territory never developed beyond the "formative" level. In this and in the following chapter, we will consider only the Central Andean Area, which is to say the territory that includes modern-day Peru except for the wild eastern area and the area close to the highlands of Bolivia. Archaeological research has identified this region as the core of the Andean culture, the only culture that generated true states, planned cities, and centers of imperial expansion. The patterns of development in this Andean culture were quite similar to those in Mesoamerica. A slow cultural evolution began with nomadic and seminomadic hunter-gatherers during the postglacial period, some of which shifted to agriculture and the herding of Camelidae and eventually went on to form the earliest agricultural villages.

The Peruvian cultural area comprises two major geographic zones: the Andean area (traditionally called the *Sierra*) and an area running along the western slope of the Cordillera overlooking the Pacific Ocean, which is referred to as the *Costa*. The area running along the eastern slope of the Cordillera where forest vegetation begins to appear is generally called the *Montaña* by the Peruvians, to distinguish it from the Amazonian forest in areas of lower elevation. To the north, the Sierra comprises three different mountain chains: the Western Cordillera (which includes the magnificent Cordillera Blanca, the highest peaks of which rise to 6,700 m./22,000 ft.), the Central Cordillera, and the Eastern Cordillera. To the south, these chains diminish from three to two until they encounter a highland with an average altitude ranging from 3,500 to 4,000 meters (11,500 to 13,000 ft.) at about the latitude of Bolivia.

Peru is decidedly in the tropics (between 4° and 18° south of the equator), but its elevation and proximity to the cold Humboldt Current running along the Pacific coast ensure a generally temperate climate. The landscape of the high Andes is semi-arid, with scanty vegetation and few trees. Rain falls chiefly during the summer months (from November to May) and is heavier to the north. The rivers, which originate in the snows of the Cordilleras, run first through the higher valleys, and then descend toward the Amazonian region (Urubamba, Huallaga, Marañón, and others), with the sole exception of the river Santa, which flows toward the Pacific.

Given the specific climatic conditions, early Andean agriculture was most prosperous. The favored crops in the valleys included maize, beans, squash, and the like; farmers in the highlands raised potatoes and quinoa and herded llamas and alpacas. Cultivation of the steep mountain slopes require terracing and systems of irrigation.

Because the ocean waters are extremely cold in this region, there is little evaporation and hence little rainfall, so the coastal strip is mostly desert. In the western Cordillera, however, more than thirty rivers have created oases in the valleys through which they run that have supported farming ever since the Preceramic period. Major pre-Columbian cultural groups settled in these valleys, and the prevailing climatic conditions have preserved a remarkable wealth of archaeological material. The climate is temperate with only minor variations throughout the year except for periodic disturbances that occur when the El Niño Current moves the Humboldt Current further out to sea. This phenomenon produces heavy rains, flooding, reductions in the fish population, and plagues of insects.

Communities in the various areas organized systems of irrigation to facilitate the cultivation of land at medium and high altitudes. They raised a variety of plants, including maize, different sorts of beans, squash, chili peppers, and tropical fruit — which, like manioc and potatoes, originally came from the eastern slopes of the Andes. Another exceedingly important agricultural product was cotton, a classic commercial crop of the Peruvian coast. In addition to these agricultural products, seafood constituted an important part of the diet for the inhabitants of the entire western area of South America. They also made good use of guano (composed principally of the excrement of the large populations of seabirds that live permanently in various places along the coast and on nearby islands) for fertilizer and fuel.

The northern boundary of the Peruvian cultural area coincides approximately with the northern border of modern Peru. To the north lies Ecuador, which has slightly different geographical features, especially along the Pacific coast. To the east, the enormous Amazonian basin is home to a culture radically different from that in the Andean area (although contacts between the two cultures did occur). To the south, the border is less sharply defined.

The origin and development of the Andean area is closely linked to the terrain and the considerable food resources. Increases in population in the more

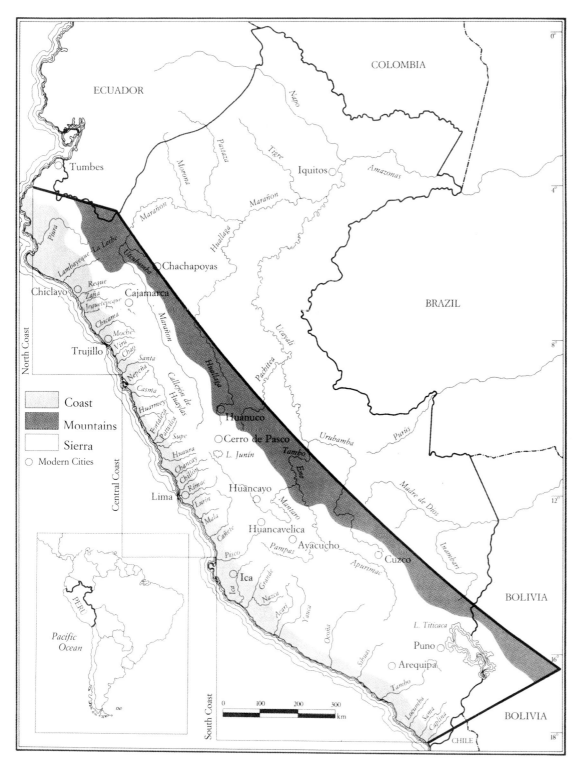

Peruvian archaeological and cultural area with environmental divisions.

favorable areas (the valleys and coastal oases) produced a number of small kingdoms, which were initially governed by groups of shamanistic priests. Archaeologists are still trying to interpret the significance of this complex cultural process, but the close relationship between humans and their physical environment is clearly a key part of the puzzle. In fact, one of the most important characteristics of the inhabitants of the Andes is the way in which they have always felt perfectly integrated with nature and hence felt themselves to be part of the divine nature.

Following pages: Desert zone of Nazca, Peru. (Photograph by Orefici)

Region of Cuzco with the snow-laden slopes of the Eastern Cordillera. (Photograph by Mireille Vautier)

137

The History of the Research

THE CULTURE OF the latest Andean phase — the Incan empire — has been well known or at least popularly recognized since the days of the Spanish conquest. The existence and character of the pre-Incan cultures, on the other hand, came to light only in the last years of the nineteenth century, through the efforts of the pioneering archaeologist Max Uhle. Using his own system, based on stratigraphic and typological evidence, Uhle identified four distinct periods of Andean culture: an Ancient period of regional cultures (the cultures we now call Mochica and Nazca); a Middle period, marked by the highlands culture of Tiahunanco and the cultures that descended from it; a Late period, characterized by the regional cultures of Chimú, Chancay, and Ica; and, lastly, the Incan period. This outline was perfected over the course of several decades, with the addition of new cultural groups and, above all, with an initial period of expansion deriving from Chavín. This great temple complex of the Sierra was brought to the attention of historians

everywhere by Julio C. Tello, the director for many years of the National Museum of Archaeology in Lima. Tello also made other important discoveries, such as that of the great temples of Sechín and Moxeque in the valley of Casma, and he studied the necropolises of Paracas on the southern coast, attributing them to the Chavín cultural complex and the Nazca culture. Another scholar, Rafael Larco Hoyle, worked chiefly on the northern coast, where he discovered evidence of Chavín influence in the necropolis of Cupinisque.

In 1946, a group of U.S. archaeologists carried out an intensive study of one of the valleys of the northern coast (Virú). Their work confirmed the established chronological sequence but added two additional stages — "Preceramic agriculture" *(Huaca Prieta)* and "initial ceramics," both of which were prior to Chavín. These stages led to the development of an Andean "Formative period," which gathered together the earliest ceramic phases with those of Chavín and the groups that derived from

Chronological scheme of the Andean Cultures (according to L. Laurencich Minelli).

Chronological Sketch of Peru

		COAST			PLATEAUS			
		North	Center	South	North	Center	South (Cuzco)	Extreme South
Horizon III	1534 1463	Inca-Chimù	Inca	Inca	Inca-Cajamarca	Inca	Inca	Inca
Higher Intermediate Period	1000	Chimù	Chancay (Cuismancu)	Chincha	Cajamarca-Huari	Huari	Pre-Inca	Tribù Aymara
Horizon II	600	Mochica-Huari	Pachacamaci-Huari	Pacheco-Huari	Huari Cajamarca III	Huari	Huari	Tiahuanaco IV
Lower Intermediate Period	200d.C. 200	Mochica Mochica e Virù	Regno di Lima Boño de Boza e M.	Nasca Nasca-Paracas Necropolis	Cajamarca III Cajamarca e Recuay	Huari	Huari Pucarà	Tiahuanaco III
Horizon I	1200	Salinar-Virù Chavín	Tracce Chavín	Paracas Cavernas	Chavín	Chavín-Kotosh		Tiahuanaco I-II Tiahuanaco I
Initial Higher	1800	Huaca Negra Las Aldas Huaca Prieta	La Florida Sito Tranque	Sito Hacha		Kotosh IV Kotosh III		
Initial Lower Preceramic	2500 3500 5000 7-6000	Huaca Prieta Playa Culebras	Asia Paraiso-Rio Seco Yacht Club Chilca	Cabezas Largas		Kotosh II Kotosh I Lauricocha III Lauricocha II		
Higher Stone	8000 11-11000	Chivateros II Chivateros I				Lauricocha I Guitarrero	Pikimachay	
Lower Stone	12000 20000	Chivateros R. Z.					Pikimachay	

Bas-relief of the Crossed Hands,
Kotosh (Huánaco, Peru).

Raw embossed clay, Preceramic epoch.
Anthropomorphic figurine from
Kotosh (Huánaco, Peru). Raw clay,
Preceramic epoch.

Chavín. The exact chronology of this development was not established until 1950, with the use of radiocarbon dating. As in the case of the Mexican Preclassic period, the new dating method gave a significantly earlier date for beginning of Chavín culture than previous estimates, pushing it back to the period from 900 to 700 B.C.E. There has been a great deal of scholarly discussion of the fact that there is a certain stylistic similarity between Chavín culture and the distant Olmec culture of Meso-america, but as yet there is no consensus on its significance.

In the years since, J. Rowe's studies in the valley of Ica, F. Engel and E. Lanning's surveys along the central Peruvian coast, and the contributions of other researchers such as R. Ravines and D. Bonavia have greatly increased our knowledge concerning the structure of the various periods and the chronology of pre-Incan Peruvian prehistory. A. Cardich and his colleagues have helped to cast additional light on the phase of the earliest hunter-gatherers. And Luis Lumbreras deserves special recognition for his work on the ruins of Chavín (with H. Amat) and on the "Tihuanacoid" city of Huari in the Ayacucho region.

Our knowledge grows daily, and the cultures of the Central Andes are revealing a complexity and a chronological depth that were quite unsuspected even just a few decades ago. For this reason, the presentation of the formative Peruvian cultures in the following pages will necessary be somewhat sketchy. We will take a closer look at the Chavín culture, giving special attention to the site, its art, and its symbolism.

*Reconstruction and excavations carried
out in the context of the "Nazca
project," sponsored by the Italian Center
for Pre-Columbian Archaeological Study
and Research of Brescia, which, under
the leadership of Giuseppe Orefici, has
seen the participation of Peruvian and
European archaeologists.*

3 Preceramic Villages and Temples

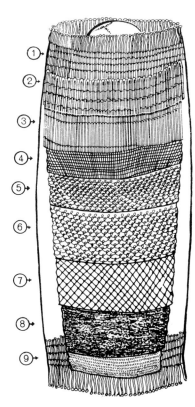

Schematic depiction of the wrappings of a funerary shroud from the Preceramic cemetery of Paracas (Precotton period, 3000 B.C.E.). (1) Cape made of plaited reeds; (2) Mat made of plaited reeds; (3) Mat made of plaited reeds; (4) Plaited cloth made from spun cactus fibers; (5) Knotted cloth made from plant fibers; (6) More knotted cloth made of plant fibers; (7) Netting made of plant fibers; (8) Vicuña hide; (9) Another hide of the same sort — the leather enclosed the body. The order shown is from the surface of the shroud toward the body (according to Engel).

THE FOUNDATION of Peruvian civilization dates back to the Preceramic Cotton period typical of the northern and central coasts of Peru. Although there are still some doubts about the exact chronology of that period, archaeologists are certain that the earliest ceremonial sites had appeared by 2200 B.C.E. The exceptional conditions of the soil in the arid coastal strip (so free of moisture as to preserve even the most perishable of materials) has made it possible for us to reconstruct the remarkable sequence of innovations and cultural development that took place there during the centuries in question.

A culture that developed in the coastal region from Las Haldas in the north to the site known as Asia in the south between 2500 and 1500 B.C.E. appears to be the original source of a number of features that distinguished later periods, some of which also appeared in the highlands to the north. These features included ceremonial temples and platforms; various constructions made of stone, adobe, and mud; the use of funerary sacks to preserve the bodies of the deceased; multiple interments, reflecting the practice of sacrificing individuals of lesser importance to accompany more important personages in their voyage to the afterworld; trophy heads; ceremonial caches; containers, tubes, and wooden boards that were used to store and ingest coca; looms and shuttles; objects for everyday use made of bone, wood, gourd, stone, and clay; bone flutes; earrings; and a great quantity of artifacts such as cordage, baskets, mats, bits of stone used as beads, and the like. There is also evidence that a considerable exchange of foodstuffs took place between the highlands and lowlands, while the exchange of manufactured products was rare.

The earliest known temple constructions on the central coast were uncovered at the sites of Río Seco and Chuquitanta (2000-1800 B.C.E.), the second of which underwent various modifications over the course of the centuries that followed. It is clear that this area supported a lower population density than sites further north, which would seem to suggest that the construction and maintenance of these sites would have required the assistance of persons from other nearby locations. Thus there must have existed some sort of organization of communities and hierarchical organization of labor. In these sites, as in Mesoamerica and other parts of the world, the construction of temples presupposes the existence of a powerful priestly elite that was responsible for directing life in the society.

Along the Peruvian coast, the food necessary for the sustenance of fixed communities must have come mostly from the sea. Indeed, these resources, available all year round, would have come close to being sufficient on their own to support a sedentary

way of life with only small additions from hunting and gathering in the early phase of light agriculture. Life in these communities was rendered richer still with later developments in the manufacture of textiles and, above all, trade between the Sierra and the Coast.

The process of cultural development might well be considered complete at this point, but the complexity of the ceremonial centers and structures continued to increase over the course of the Initial Ceramic period. This would seem to indicate that the priestly groups were acquiring greater power and prestige during this period. Villages extended over much of the Central Andean Area, though we do not know whether or not that was a consequence of this phenomenon. Temple structures appeared on the northern coast and in the high Andes valleys, reaching as far as some zones of the central coast such as Las Haldas (situated atop an ocean promontory). At La Florida, on the outskirts of the modern city of Lima, the remains of a great step pyramid have been uncovered. It was built not with sun-dried bricks, as was the custom on the coast, but with stones cemented together with a mixture of mud and plaster. There were other constructions and courtyards at the foot of the temple. This site undoubtedly constituted the focal point of the villages scattered along the river Rímac. As time passed, some sites were abandoned (e.g., Río Seco) and other sites sprang up (e.g., Ancón). At a number of sites, buildings or larger orderly plazas were built on the upper section of a rocky spur or hill. One such site was Las Haldas, to the south of the valley of Casma, where an odd, low-standing, oval structure was built. The location of this ceremonial complex — which measures 650 × 200 meters (2,130 × 656 ft.), without counting the huge landfill set at the entrance to the complex — may have had some connection with the ancient cult of *Mama-Cocha* (the primordial waters represented by the ocean), a cult that was still active at the time of the Spanish conquest.

In the Sierra, the best known complex is that of Kotosh, dating from the Final Preceramic period (the "Myth Phase") and is set at an altitude of nearly two thousand meters (6,560 ft.) above sea level, overlooking a tributary of the Hallaga River. The excavations, conducted by archaeologists from the University of Tokyo, have led to the discovery of three temples, one set atop the other, which date from the Preceramic period (approximately 2000 1800 B.C.E.), and two other temples, which date from the Initial Ceramic period: all of them were thus built prior to the arrival of Chavín influences. Another similar structure has been found near the site of Toril in Callejón de Huaylas. This site pre-

144

sents noteworthy similarities to the Templo de las Manos Cruzadas (Temple of the Crossed Hands) at Kotosh, which was built in the same way, atop a tall platform.

It is noteworthy that the introduction of ceramics had no special influence on the development of these areas. In this context, ceramics serve as just one more indicator of a social and cultural movement that developed over the course of the second millennium B.C.E. and that was contemporary with the cultivation and consumption of maize and the beginning of the construction of a system of irrigation canals through the valleys. We do not know whether these innovations were necessitated by the pressures of population growth or whether the increase in population was made possible by these innovations. We do know, however, that from the middle of this millennium onward, the foundations were being laid for an organization typical of a proto-state, apparently structured in small independently operating groups directed by a proto-priestly class that acquired greater influence over time.

The fact that the morphology and development of the temple cores was not uniform indicates the existence of a series of divergent traditions of ideology and ritual. In the coastal region, two types of constructions have been identified. One featured a relatively tall platform set behind a sunken courtyard that was rectangular or circular in shape. The second construction featured two or three stacked platforms set at the end of a courtyard that was bounded by two lateral building structures. The whole complex was thus assembled in the shape of a U, which was characteristically oriented northward or northeastward — in the direction of the Cordillera, which was held to be the origin and provenance of all water, the source of life for the valleys.

Further inland, five sites have been found at elevations ranging from 1,000 to 3,800 meters (3,280 to 12,465 ft.). Among this group is the site of Kotosh, mentioned previously, near which it is still possible to see the remains of the temple of Shillacoto, which was used as a burial site during the Initial Ceramic period. The fundamental feature of the temples in this group is the presence of a rectangular chamber with a floor set on two levels, one centered inside the other. The central floor space served as a hearth, a space for ceremonial fire that was held to be sacred to the gods. Various types of offerings were burnt here. Other sites incorporate variants on these typologies that probably reflect a process of development and evolution. Some of the structures are circular rather than rectangular, for instance, or feature a floor-level rather than sunken central hearth; some rectangular constructions with sunken hearths omit the roof; some keep the roof

and incorporate a system of lateral ventilation for the hearth (e.g., the Templo de las Manos Cruzadas at Kotosh). This group of sites is considered representative of a Kotosh religious tradition, the principal manifestation of which was the worship of fire, as opposed to water cults that were more typical of the religious tradition of the coast.

Drawing of the Temple of Crossed Hands and the White Temple, Kotosh (Huánaco, Peru).

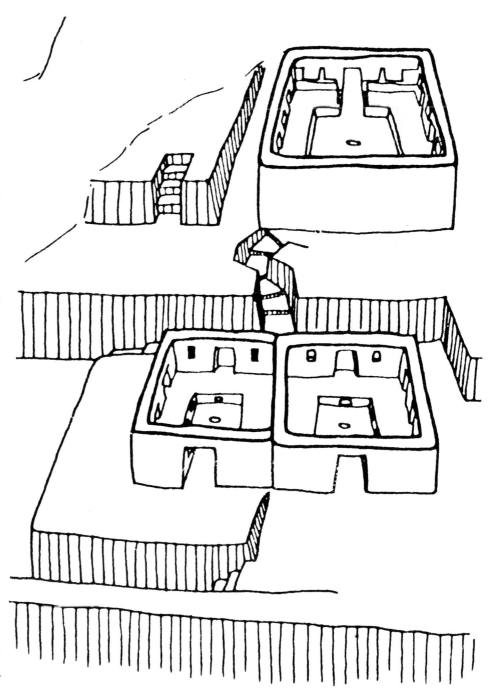

Top: *Drawing of a splendid receptacle made out of a large gourd, hollowed out, with decorations engraved on the rind. From Huaca Prieta, on the northern coast of Peru.*

Bottom: *Depiction of a condor with a serpent on its chest, obtained through the dyeing of cotton fabric. From Huaca Prieta.*

Right: *Desert shoals in the Peninsula of Paracas, in southern Peru.*
(Photograph by Mireille Vautier)

146

4 The Temples of the Valley of Casma

Drawing of a stela of Cerro Sechín. The bas-relief depicts the personage known as the "Pontiff of Sacrifices" (according to Kauffmann Doig).

Map of the temple complexes of Sechín Alto and Cerro Sechín in the valley of Casma.
(Redrawn by J. Ferrari according to indications given by Tello)

IF THE LAS HALDAS complex is the most noteworthy site from the final Preceramic and early Ceramic periods, the temple of Sechín in the valley of Casma is the most spectacular site from the intermediate phase of the Initial Ceramic period (also known as the Ancient Formative period). Recent studies indicate that an earthen platform lined with stones — about 40 meters (130 ft.) tall, 300 meters (985 ft.) long, and 250 meters (820 ft.) wide — was built around 1400 B.C.E., at the site known as Sechín Alto. A U-shaped ceremonial center was built on this platform, oriented in a northeasterly direction — indicating that it was a larger and more complex version of the similar structures on the Peruvian coast. Other smaller buildings surrounded the site.

A separate group, featuring a rectangular structure that was subdivided into a number of different spaces, was built, half a century later at the foot of Cerro Sechín, some 1,500 meters (4,920 ft.) south of Sechín Alto. Archaeologists have identified four phases of construction at the Cerro Sechín site. On both sides of the northern stairway there are representations of giant fish, about 3.7 meters (12 ft.) in length; they are painted and engraved. Other representations are evident on the interior, but they are, sadly, in very poor condition. During an extensive renovation and enlargement conducted around 1300 B.C.E., workers added the "Platform of Engraved Plaques," a collection of strange engravings

on slabs of stone of various sizes attached to the outer wall. Figures of warriors armed with "head trophy" maces alternate with scenes of bodies cut open and other drawings that might well be depictions of bones and viscera. Several scholars maintain that these depictions might have been made in the wake of a particularly bloody invasion of people from the Sierra. A more accepted hypothesis is that the engravings were made in the course of a major agricultural expansion in the valley and depict fertility rites that involved human sacrifice. In any case, it appears that this long frieze once entirely covered the side walls and was designed to strike terror into into the hearts of participants in religious rites.

It was once believed that the art of Cerro Sechín was contemporary with or possibly later than the art of Chavín, but it has been determined that it is actually earlier than Olmec art (1250 B.C.E.). The ceremonial platform of Sechín Alto was a clear forerunner of the great mound of San Lorenzo, by about 150 years. One wonders how it could have been possible to organize and plan the sort of collective labor that would have been necessary to undertake construction on this scale in an area that could not have housed or produced food for more that a few thousand persons. That the project was accomplished at all would seem to indicate that the representatives of this important cultural movement were warrior-priests with substantial theocratic power.

Another interesting complex is found at Pampa de las Llamas, just three kilometers (2 mi.) southeast of Sechín Alto. It is made up of a series of plazas and a *huaca,* or sacred precinct, set on a number of rectangular platforms with rounded corners, the lowest of which measures 160 meters (525 ft.) in diameter. The complex is known as the Temple of Mojeque, from the name of the river that flows nearby. Here, too, there is a central stairway that leads to an elevated courtyard, behind which are two even higher platforms, upon which it is likely there once stood a number of small temples built out of perishable materials. The vertical wall of the third base platform was punctuated by a row of great "idols" modeled in clay — reliefs standing roughly three meters (10 ft.) in height depicting human figures. Over time, these were defaced: the lower extremities were mutilated and the heads were broken off and have disappeared. The site is clearly as old as Cerro Sechín, and it is stylistically similar to that site. On two of the walls, over the bodies of the "idols," we can see a foreshadowing of what is to become a typical Chavín motif — the serpent. Scholars are uncertain about its symbolic value and function in this context, however.

To sum up, the coastal and inland areas of Peru produced at least ten centuries of ceremonial archi-

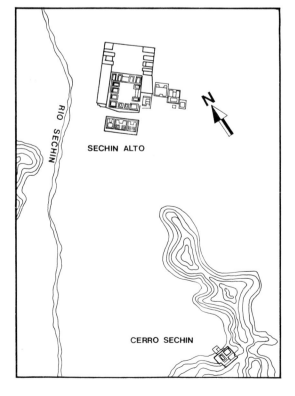

RIO SECHIN

SECHIN ALTO

N

CERRO SECHIN

The temple of Cerro Sechín according to Tello's reconstruction.

Following double-page spread:
Reconstruction of the first phase of construction of the ceremonial center of Chavín de Huantar.

tecture. The site of Chavín clearly did not spring from a void, nor did it constitute the sole driving force of the earliest great Andean artistic style. Rather, Chavín was a great center of the late period that gathered, developed, and expanded on previ- ous experimentation of all sorts, performing a bril- liant synthesis and developing, in a monumental and highly baroque form, concepts and practices of shamanistic origin that had first been developed during the late Preceramic period.

Plan and cross-sections of the Temple of Mojeque. (according to Kauffmann Doig).

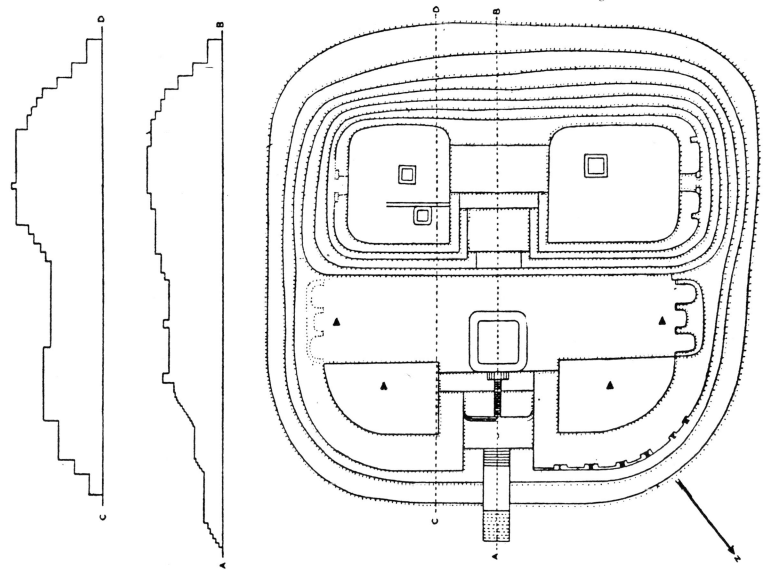

5 The Culture of Chavín: The Lanzón

AROUND 900 B.C.E. or slightly thereafter, an unknown group of people built a U-shaped temple opening eastward with stones transported from nearby hills. This structure, which measured more than 100 meters (330 ft.) in length, constituted the earliest example of a building of monumental size in the Peruvian Sierra. Not far from where this building now stands in ruins is the modern-day village of Chavín de Huantar (3,150 m./10,330 ft. above sea level), which gave its name to the site. The typically Andean geography of this site consists of a valley set to the east of the Cordillera Blanca and cut by the river Mosna, which runs northeast toward the valley of the river Marañón. A mountain pass, twenty kilometers (about 12 mi.) west of Chavín, at an elevation of 4,600 meters (15,090 ft.), provides communication between the site and the nearby Callejón de Huaylas.

On the western slopes of the Cordillera is Huaricoto, one of the earliest temples of the north-central Sierra. This site was first occupied around the third millennium B.C.E., although its ceremonial enclosure (with a central hearth set on a sunken floor, similar to the structure found at Kotosh) was built during a later period. It was also occupied during the Initial Ceramic period (Toril phase), but it was not a stylistic forerunner of Chavín.

In fact there are no known antecedents for Chavín in the recently studied ruins of the temple of Piruru along the course of the river Marañón. How can we explain the arrival of such a magnificent and sizable temple complex in such an unfrequented and hard-to-reach location? In all likelihood, Chavín was a center for astronomical and calendrical observations, but this alone does not

suffice to explain its out-of-the-way location. A more credible explanation is undoubtedly linked to the Andean belief system concerning the "sacred landscape." Some seventeen kilometers (11 mi.) away north by northwest is the Nevado de Huantsan (6,395 m./20,976 ft. above sea level), a mountain of the Cordillera Blanca that was believed in ancient times to be the home of Andean deities that guard and control the region. This mountain is also the source of a stream called the Wacheksa that flows into the river Mosna. The water of this stream was considered sacred, and the shamans took readings of the disposition of the gods from the sound of the rushing water. Architects of Chavín diverted some of the water from the Wacheksa to flow through underground channels that run through the ceremonial complex. The principal use of these channels, therefore, was not practical (e.g., for irrigation or for cooling the rooms) but sacred (for use in the discernment of omens). It is believed, in fact, that the channels amplified the sounds of the waters that rushed during the summer thaws, producing a roar similar to that of the jaguar, and that this special sound was the foundation for certain oracular and initiatory practices. Indeed, although the site had long been abandoned by the time of the Spanish conquest, Chavín was still described as a major "place of oracles."

Chavín is located between two mountains that the indigenous population still considers to be inhabited by spirits. One is Pojoc (4,260 m./13,973 ft. tall), upon which a sanctuary dedicated to Mama Rayhuana still stands; the other, to the east, is Huacac (4,470 m./14,662 ft. tall). Chavín is at the apex of the valley that opens out northeastward between

Plan of the ceremonial center of Chavín de Huantar. (according to Kauffmann Doig).
1. *Late temple, known as "El Castillo"*
2. *Central section of the ancient temple*
3. *One of the buildings that stood adjacent to the ancient temple*
4. *Sunken square of the ancient temple*
5. *Location of the Lanzón, inside the subterranean tunnels*

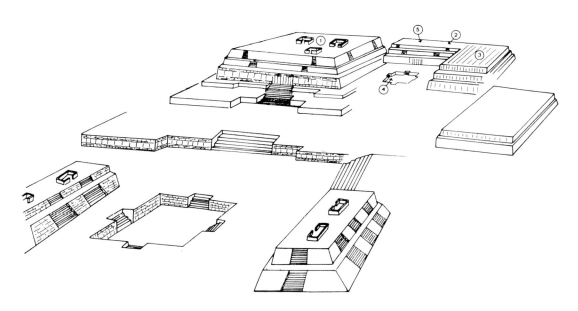

The eastern façade of El Castillo, Chavín de Huantar (Ancash, Peru).

them in the direction of the Marañón River basin. The artists of Chavín, who were quite expert in symbolic and naturalistic iconography, drew considerable inspiration from a forest that begins at a three-day's march from the site. As we have already noted, the Pacific slope of the range contains a pass that has been in use since ancient times leading to the valley of the river Santa and thus Callejón de Huaylas by way of the Cordillera Negra through the valleys of Nepeña and Casma. The location of Chavín is thus strategic in many ways — in terms of economics and communications but also religion and symbolism. It is here that the highest and most magnificent sector of the Peruvian Andes intersects with the road that joins the eastern world to the western world, the life of the rain forest with that of the great ocean that bathes the desert. The symbol of this union can be found in two galleries inside the Ancient Temple of Chavín; the galleries are oriented according to the four cardinal points of the compass, and at their center is the great stone *Lanzón*, which serves as the axis mundi.

The Lanzón is a monolith that has been completely carved. Viewed from either the right or the left, it affords a profile in accordance with the stylistic typology of Chavín. The same figure is carefully engraved and subdivided on both sides of the stone. The head of the individual is square and initially appears anthropomorphic; the corners of the mouth, upturned, give the image the appearance of a "smiling deity." In all other aspects, however, the figure is rigid and menacing: the eyes are wide open and have the distinctive appearance of birds' eyes characteristic of other depictions of the Chavín typology. Further up, two serpents curve over the eyebrows. The deity is adorned with earrings made of two associated elements — a ring attached to a wide support piece attached to the ear. The nose is typically Chavín, and two tusks jut from the mouth, pointing upward. An arm ending in five fingers and a leg ending in five claws (which might be either avian or feline) are carved on either side of the figure. Different positioning of the arms constitutes the only break in the symmetry between the two sides: the right arm is raised, while the left arm hangs down. In place of hair, the deity has a welter of serpents. Other depictions, in part independent of the main figure, complete the decoration of the monolith.

Carved on a block of granite 4.6 meters (15 ft.) tall, the Lanzón is a sort of *menhir* or *huaca* — a sacred place. Its pointed bottom is fitted into a hole that was specially drilled into the floor; the top supports the ceiling of the passageway in which it stands. This is a major cosmic, natural, and human symbol, with clearly monstrous features. Its location suggests that it was probably the last image the priests had to face in the initiation process. Some scholars believe that it may be a prototypical version of the Andean creator god Huiracocha.

On the interior of the ancient temple of Chavin de Huantar, at the intersection of two galleries, stands the Lanzón, so called because of its spear shape. The stone monolith stands some 4.6 meters (15 ft.) tall and is set in a special hole drilled into the flooring.

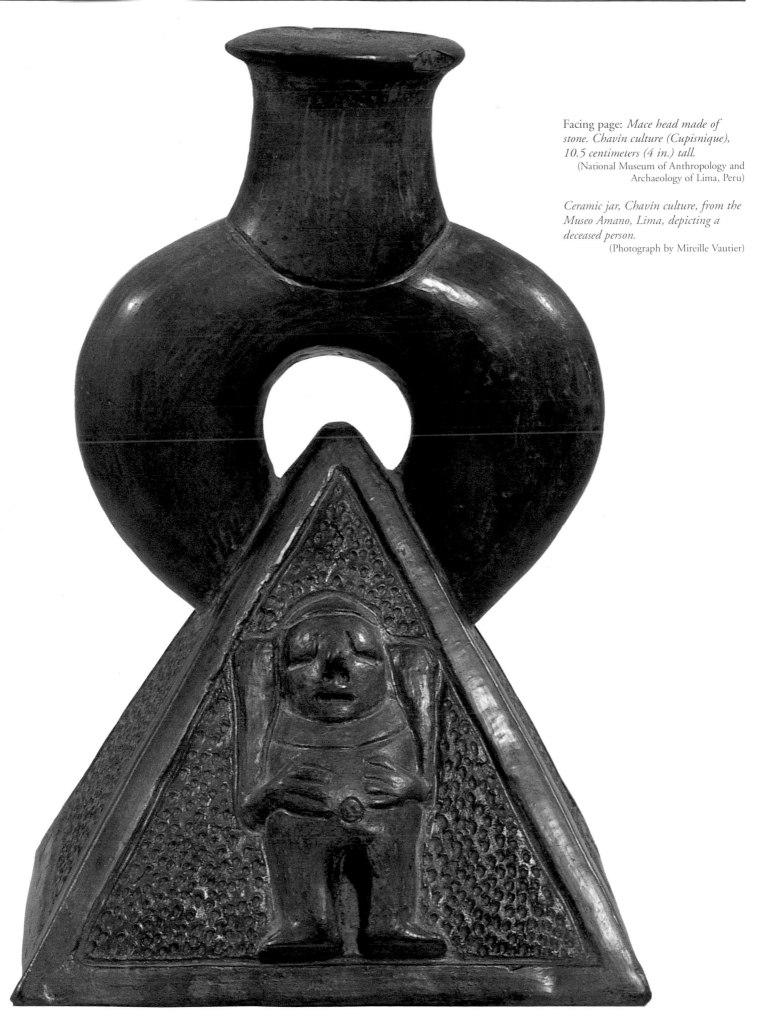

Facing page: *Mace head made of stone. Chavín culture (Cupisnique), 10.5 centimeters (4 in.) tall.*
(National Museum of Anthropology and Archaeology of Lima, Peru)

Ceramic jar, Chavín culture, from the Museo Amano, Lima, depicting a deceased person.
(Photograph by Mireille Vautier)

6 The Culture of Chavín: The Art

Drawing of the famous Raimondi Stela, attributed to the late phase of the Chavín culture. It is 1.95 meters (6 ft.) tall and 75 centimeters (2.5 ft.) wide. It probably formed part of a courtyard or stood at the entrance door of a ceremonial enclosure.

THE ANCIENT TEMPLE of Chavín is a monumental version of sanctuaries that have existed in the coastal region ever since the Initial Ceramic period. It incorporates a number of distinctive architectural features in the tradition of those sanctuaries, including a circular sunken courtyard fronting the temple that can be reached via four broad stairways. The courtyard is lined with stelae carved with depictions of humans, predatory birds, and felines.

Not long after the construction of the Ancient Temple had been completed, when the power of the chief priestly group had already been adequately consolidated, it appears that a proto-state developed and that Chavín became its ceremonial and administrative center. The outskirts of the new open city were populated by craftspeople, merchants, and peasants. During this period, the Temple was expanded southward. Archaeologists refer to this enlargement as the "New Temple"; the Spanish conquerors dubbed it *El Castillo* ("the Castle"). The new construction also included the addition of a network of underground tunnels. The upper platform of the New Temple, which was probably occupied by a number of small temples that have since disappeared, was accessed by a stairway. In front of the temple, a small rectangular courtyard opened onto a large plaza, on either side of which stood lateral buildings. At the center of this large plaza was another sunken courtyard, thirty meters (100 ft.) wide.

The remains of the external walls, still in evidence, have taught us a good deal about the building techniques used by the architects of El Castillo. Unlike the Cyclopean structures erected by the Incas, this structure was made up of rows of large rectangular stones cemented together with a clay-based amalgam. Several tenoned sculpted heads — sculptures mixing human and feline features — were driven into the outer wall.

The ruins have also yielded valuable stone artifacts, many quite large, the original placement of which remains a matter of speculation. One of these is the Tello obelisk, a column with a rectangular cross-section standing about 2.5 meters (8 ft.) tall, the upper section of which is tapered, much like the Lanzón. The four sides of the obelisk are covered with an intricate pattern of designs; among them one can distinguish the form of a crocodile or cayman. This iconography is repeated, with minor variations, along the surface of both the two larger sides and the smaller sides. Above the crocodile are small designs of human beings, feline heads, serpents, and seashells. The upper section features a bird, a fish, and a cat that appear to be emerging from the crocodile's head. Alongside this is a cross with a circle at the center; a smaller version of the cross is visible at the height of the crocodile's neck.

The cross-shaped sign is common in the symbology of Chavín and of Andean cultures in general. In this case, it is an ancient manifestation of the tetravalent conception of time and space. A number of plants that are sculpted on the smaller sides of the obelisk were probably sacred in nature and may have possessed hallucinogenic powers. Another stela does include a character holding a plant identifiable as a "cactus of St. Pedro." This and other evidence indicate that these plants were used in the shamanistic rites of Chavín.

Another extremely important find was the Raimondi Stela, named in honor of the French archaeologist who found it beneath the floor of a peasant's house and arranged for it to be moved to Lima. Considered to be a later work than the Lanzón and the Tello obelisk, the Raimondi Stela depicts a personage face-on adorned with complex ornamental accessories. The stela may have formed part of the decoration of a courtyard or the entrance to a ceremonial enclosure. It stands almost two meters (6.5 ft.) tall and seventy-five centimeters (2.5 ft.) wide.

The Raimondi Stela is so elaborate that a thorough description would be very lengthy. Its principal features include two faces with feline features (one face is right-side up and the other is upside-down), an enormous extension atop the head in which it is possible to make out three feline heads, and feet with talons like those of a predatory bird. The whole figure is covered with serpent-shaped elements. Both sides of the stela feature eight serpents associated with lines in the form of clubs. Kauffmann Doig has suggested that these could be metaphors for plumes in the complex hairdressing of a "tiger-striped angel" that appears on columns outside the entrance of the "New Temple." There is really too little information available concerning the mind-set and sensibilities of the architects of these monuments to make any sound interpretations of this symbolism, however. All we can say with certainty is that the clubs were held to be sacred and that they doubtless served some specific ceremonial function, as in the rites of initiation.

The deity of the clubs on the Raimondi Stela does seem to be an antecedent to the central personage on the Gate of the Sun of Tiahuanaco; as such it would have even stronger ties than the Lanzón to the eventual development of Huiracocha. The issue of specific influence is knotty, however. Many scholars have perceived an iconographic similarity between the art of Chavín and that of the prehistoric Olmecs. The two cultures were contemporary with each other, and each is considered to be the "mother" culture of a vast American expanse. Are these perceived similarities a product of chance or the result of contact and reciprocal influence? If the latter, which influenced which? Could there be shared Asiatic roots, the product of trans-Pacific migration, as Betty Meggers has suggested in connection with the Olmec culture? Or are the perceived similarities nothing more than the fruit of a convergence brought about by parallel perceptions of archetypal forces? The problem is open to debate and will probably remain so for quite some time.

The art of Chavín manifests itself chiefly in the architecture and stone monuments of the Chavín site, and yet it also comprises ceramic art and other artifacts from the coastal sites. Udima and Alto de la Guitarras, among other sites, have yielded a number of interesting examples of rock art. The most important ceramic finds of Chavín have been made in several of the interior galleries in El Castillo. Another important ceramic style, known as Cupinisque (from the name of the place where R. Larco Hoyle found a tomb containing the most impressive known examples), exhibits extremely fine workmanship. The style is monochrome, with decorations that are variously engraved and molded, the most typical forms being globe-shaped amphorae with narrow necks and pouring vases with stirrup handles. The latter of these forms was already represented in Machalilla ceramics from Ecuador dated 1400 to 1000 B.C.E. and in ceramics from the Mesoamerican site of Tlatilco for a brief period around 1000 B.C.E. This similarity also raises the question of whether there were contacts between Andean and Mesoamerican cultures. The Chavín stirrup pottery appears to have originated in Cupinisque (especially in the northern coastal region) and spread from there, surviving until the late Chimú period. In all of these artifacts, we find the curvilinear style and motifs typical of the Chavín school of art.

Drawing of the Tello Obelisk. A complex set of figures, among them a caiman, is engraved on both of the main sides.

Stone mortar in the shape of a jaguar. The spots on the hide have been replaced by crosses and other symbolic motifs. The eyes were originally covered with layers of obsidian.

Large bottle with a double-stirrup neck depicting a plant. Chavín culture.
(Chilean Museum of Pre-Columbian Art)

Plate made of engraved stone. Chavín culture.
(Chilean Museum of Pre-Columbian Art)

Above: *Overall view of the New Temple, or El Castillo, at Chavín de Huantar (Ancash, Peru).*

Far left: *Large bottle made of engraved ceramics. Chavín culture.*
(Chilean Museum of Pre-Columbian Art)

Left: *Two-faced figure depicting the human-feline. Chavín culture.*
(Chilean Museum of Pre-Columbian Art)

159

7 The Chavín Horizon

Depiction of the feline god in the Paracas culture. In the left hand, it is holding a skull trophy.

FROM THE TIME of the Ancient Temple, and especially beginning with the construction of the New Temple in the seventh century B.C.E., the Chavín style spread through the valleys of the central and northern coastal region, penetrating as far as the northern Sierra. The style is particularly evident in the temple centers of Kuntur-Huasi (Cajamarca), where monoliths and other carved stones have been found; Caballo Muerto (Valley of Moche); Cerro Blanco and Punguri in the valley of Nepeña; Pallca in the valley of Casma, which Tello described as a "typical Chavín city built on a natural platform"; Garagay Alto near Lima; and various sites of the Kotosh-Chavín phase in the central Sierra. All of these regions were directly subject to Chavín influence, in all likelihood through the formation of a proto-empire and a well-organized trading network or else through the propagation of a particularly prestigious religion. The spread of Chavín appears to have been peaceful, although there are a few isolated evidences of warfare dating from the Formative period. This culture produced no fortresses or weapons and made no forays into metallurgy beyond some work in gold, which was limited to the production of tableware, bracelets, and other embossed objects (examples of which have been found in the valley of Lambayeque).

Very little is known about the social and political structure of Chavín, but it is believed to have been a theocratic state.

In archaeological terms, Chavín can basically be defined as a "great artistic style," the first that succeeded to spread, in all its manifestations, throughout an extensive area of the central Andean region. Its influence, however, reached all the way to far northern Peru, and was especially strong on the south-central coast, where the Paracas culture originated. Paracas was known in particular for its splendid fabrics, featuring an elaborate weaving technique, striking colors, and a unique iconography that generally incorporated complex mythological figures. Particularly notable were the magnificent fabrics used to wrap the bodies of the dead. Funerary sacks were placed in special underground chambers that could be reached through a well shaft (the Cavernas phase) or interred in cemeteries, some of which contained subterranean architectural structures (the Necropolis phase).

The style of Chavín ceramics gradually evolved from a pure original style to a variety of regional styles. The most elaborate ceramic phase was connected with the Nazca culture near the beginning of the Common Era.

Chavín was the product of a brilliant cultural

Painting showing the breakdown of a funerary bundle, revealing the mummy.
(National Museum of Anthropology and Archaeology of Lima, Peru)

Like La Venta and other leading ceremonial centers, Chavín de Huantar eventually began to decline. Starting in the second century B.C.E., groups from Callejon de Huaylas began to move into the site. Shortly thereafter, the site was abandoned entirely. The mission of Chavín, however, was complete: it had inaugurated the great Andean culture.

Complex personage of the Paracas culture.

One feature of the Paracas culture is the superb art of weaving. This drawing shows a complete set of clothing from the necropolis on the peninsula of Paracas.

synthesis over long period of time. It was endowed with a force for expansion that engendered the first pan-Peruvian horizon, which brought to fruition the Formative period of the Andean culture. Chavín served as the matrix for various derivative cultural phases, such as Salinar and Virú or Gallinazo on the northern coast, and these in turn led to the development of the Mochica regional culture. Other groups arose in the Sierra, such as Huaraz and Recuay. The central coast produced the local group called Lima. The south coast produced the Paracas culture, which continued with the Nazca culture, which was renowned for its polychrome ceramics and the great inscribed anthropomorphic and zoomorphic lines.

Mochica and Nazca were the principal cultures of the Classic Andean period (also known as a time of "regional flourishing," or, more simply, as the Intermediate Ancient period). The influence of Chavín was not felt further south, however, nor in the valley of Cuzco or on the highland of Lake Titicaca, where the groups of the local Formative period enjoyed a relatively autonomous development.

Facing page: *Detail of a cape of the Paracas culture, with embroideries of mythological characters and fringe along the hems.*
(National Museum of Anthropology and Archaeology of Lima, Peru)

Large multicolored mantle of the Paracas culture featuring embroidered characters in alternating positions and colors.
(National Museum of Anthropology and Archaeology of Lima, Peru)

Colossal head of Tiahuanaco.

PART VI

The People From the Center of the World: Tiahuanaco

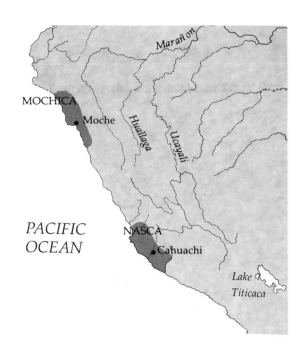

View of Sillustani, Colla culture, the ruins of which are located on a peninsula in the waters of the lagoon of Umayo.
(Photograph by Mireille Vautier)

Clay wall of the Ciudadela Tschudi at Chan Chan. Chimú culture. The friezes show mythological creatures — half quadrupeds and half birds.
(Photograph by Mireille Vautier)

The "Sun Gate" at Tiahuanaco.

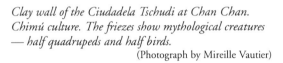

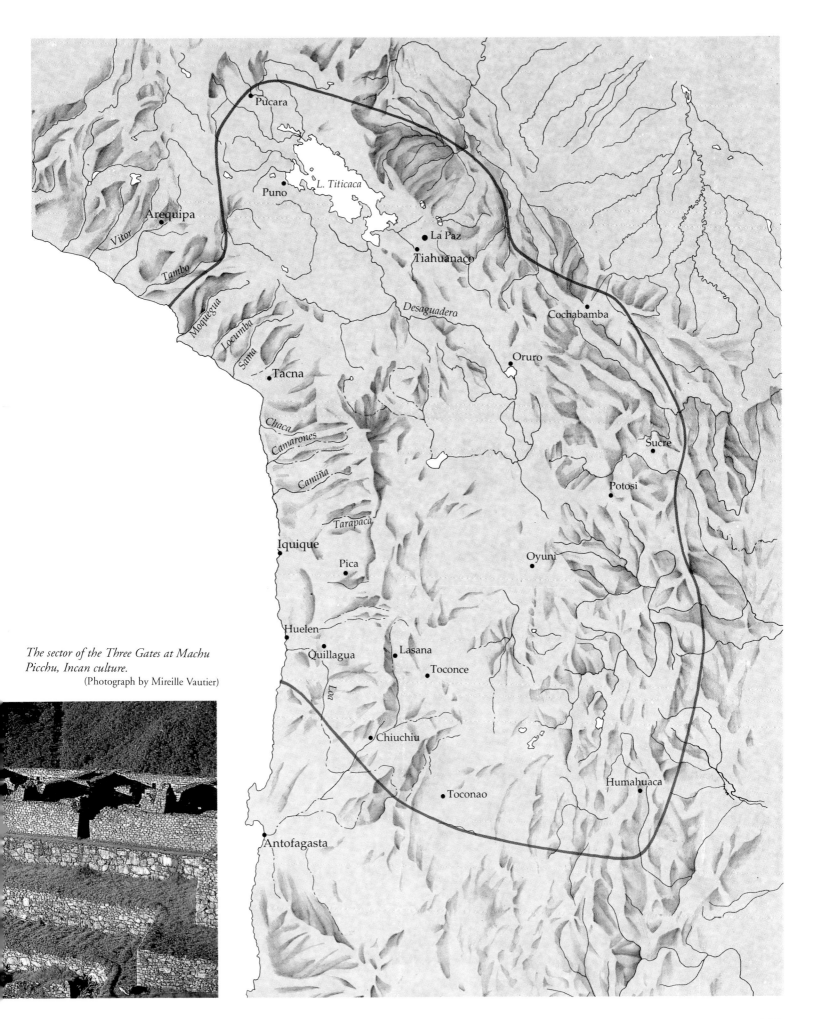

The sector of the Three Gates at Machu Picchu, Incan culture.
(Photograph by Mireille Vautier)

1 The Classic Period: Nazca and Mochica

Anthropomorphic jar from the Nazca culture, depicting a woman wearing a headdress and a lavishly decorated mantle.   (From Orefici, Nasca)

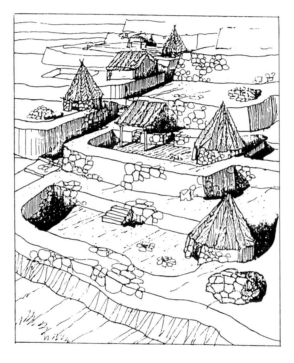

Chocholtaja (Ica): Chart of the building typologies of the Paracas-Nazca era — groups of dwellings set on complexes of andenes, or platforms (according to Williams, 1980).

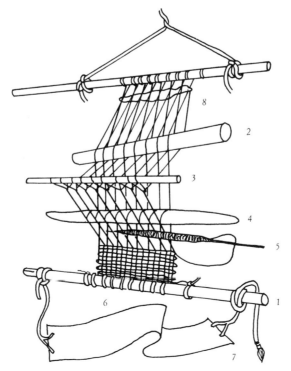

Diagram of a Nazca belt or back-strap loom.
1. Beam
2. Batten
3. Heddle
4. Shuttle
5. Weft yarn
6. Warp thread ties
7. Belt
8. Warp threads

IT IS PRACTICALLY IMPOSSIBLE, in this context, to provide a thorough treatment of all of the cultures of the Peruvian area during the Classic or Intermediate Ancient period, so we will focus on the two chief cultures of the coast, speaking in greater detail about the cultural evolution of the highlands, which was centered in Tiahuanaco.

Lastly, we will take a brief look at the Incas, the final example of the political and cultural flowering of the Sierra.

We have already noted that shortly before the beginning of the Common Era the cultures that derived from the Chavín Horizon gave way to a great many noteworthy regional subcultures. The artistic styles of these subcultures, which were expressed especially in ceramics and textiles, developed independently at the sites where surviving artifacts have been found; one might even venture to say that they have a "nationalistic" character. Although architecture continued to be mostly funerary or religious in function, it provides evidence, along with other artifacts, that point to the development of a state governed by an elite warrior priesthood. Mochica pottery, for example, frequently depicts figures wearing helmets and carrying maces.

For some seven centuries these regional groups lived in a relatively peaceful manner, after which they began to decline or to undergo rapid transformations, moving onward — to a greater or lesser degree — into the second "Pan-Peruvian Horizon," which originated with the culture of Tiahuanaco.

The population of the Peruvian area reached its greatest density during the Classic period. Irrigation systems multiplied, and the terraced land under cultivation increased considerably. New population centers sprang up, though these never quite rose to the level of planned cities. Other centers built fortifications for purposes of defense. Evidence of technological and artistic progress (principally measured by developments in architecture and especially in the construction of tombs) has led modern observers to guess that there were sharp divisions among the social classes and a distinct specialization in the crafts. Although it is regrettably the case that a great many of the tombs were ransacked by *huaqueros* (local grave robbers), one major funerary complex, in one of the adobe pyramids of the northern coast, has survived. This is the site of the "Lord of Sipan," which was discovered and subjected to scientific study only recently. The site is located in the valley of Lambayeque, and dates from about 300 C.E. The grave goods found in the tomb are particularly rich, and they reflect the Mochica style. The presence in the tomb of a great many objects made of gold indicates that the manufacture of products in this metal, which probably originated in Colombia and Ecuador, attained some importance along the northern coast as well. Along the southern coast, on the other hand, it would seem that techniques of metallurgy originated in the highlands, where the first bronze artifacts have been found, and later spread throughout the Andean region, serving as the foundation for the expansion of the culture of Tiahuanaco.

The culture of Nazca, which is believed to be a

continuation of the Paracas culture of the southern Peruvian coast, preserved various features of Chavín culture in its ceramic decorations. Nazca ceramics, which boasted an extremely high level of technical artistry and a particularly rich array of symbolic values, are especially striking for their fine finish and their use of many colors (in some cases, as many as twelve colors are used on a given artifact). Engraving and painting surpassed modeling in importance, giving evidence of a stylistic evolution that ranges from a degree of realism in the depiction of plants and animal to a high level of abstraction and symbolic complexity. Among the symbols, a deity with feline attributes and a tongue protruding from its mouth stands out in particular. In some cases, the decoration was reduced to a mere interplay of ornamentation. Nazca textiles had the same technical richness as the textiles of Paracas. The hot dry climate favored the development of a relatively simple architecture. Most of the buildings were made of *quincha* (a plant material covered with mud). There are no great temples like those in the north. Nazca appears to have conducted most of its religious ceremonies out of doors, suggesting that the religion probably had a special celestial or astral character. There is some evidence of this in the geoglyphs of the Pampa of Nazca, an array of long furrows cut into the rocky soil; these furrows sometimes intersect, forming what are presumed to be ceremonial paths, while in other cases they form huge stylized figures of animals, especially birds.

From the valleys of Moche and Chicama on the northern coast of Peru, this culture spread northward as far as the Piura area and southward as far as the valley of Santa. The Mochica developed a noteworthy architectural style based on the use of adobe that is reflected in both their dwellings and their ceremonial structures, such as the *Huaca del Sol* and the *Huaca de la Luna,* step pyramids standing at the entrance to the valley of Moche. Before they turned to farming and built great aqueducts to bring water from the Sierra to the various villages, the Mochica lived on the products of the sea. They sailed along the coast in vessels made of *totora* (like the balsas of Lake Titicaca), trading and at times making war on the local populations.

Through their ceramics, we know a great deal about the everyday activities of this people. The exceptional realism of these priceless artifacts has won the Mochica the sobriquet of "the Ancient Greeks of the Americas." Among the most remarkable of the artifacts are the portrait vases, which are so detailed as to depict the deformities and infirmities of their subjects with enough accuracy to permit modern scientist to identify their conditions. In general, Mochica pottery shows greater plasticity but a less impressive use of color than Nazca pottery. Many vases are equipped with stirrup-shaped fixtures, a typical feature inherited from the Chavín culture. Mochica artists also became skilled in the art of working precious metals after having derived the basic techniques from the northern Andean area.

Drawing of part of a Mochica vase, showing a dwelling.

Examples of Machica vase art.
Top: *A warrior capturing a prisoner.*
Above. *Weaver-women at work.*
Note the textile tools and the boards showing the patterns to be woven.
Left: *Dance of the dead beneath the stars.*

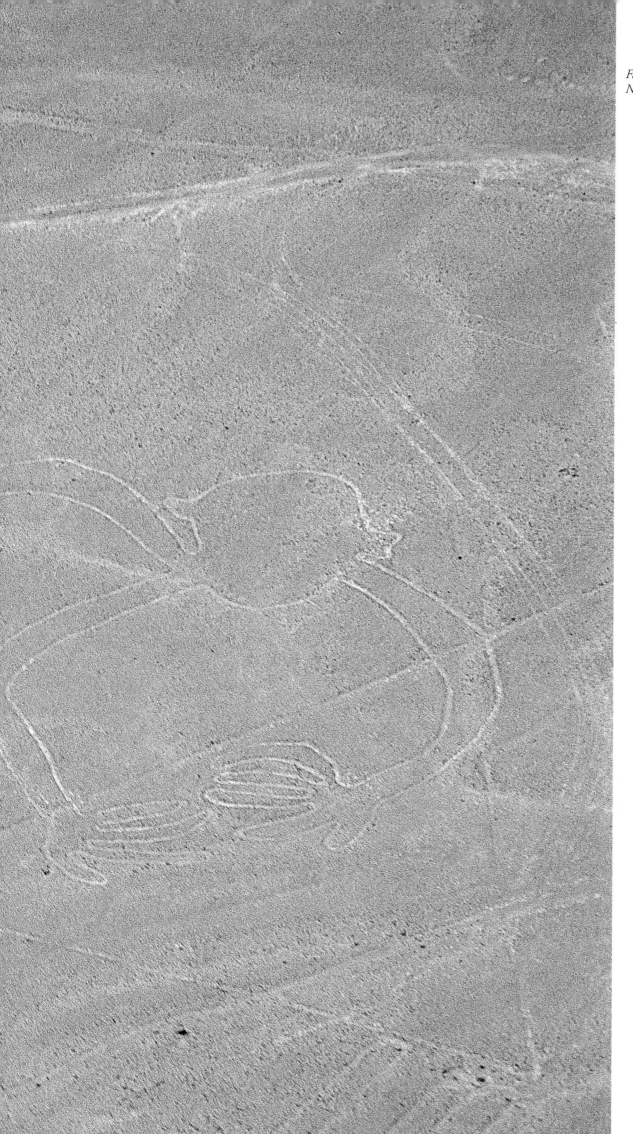

2 The Forerunners of Tiahuanaco

TIAHUANACO (also known as Tiwanaku) is the name of a small indigenous village in Bolivia located about twenty kilometers (12 mi.) south of Lake Titicaca at an elevation of 3,840 meters (12,595 ft.) above sea level. Not far from the village are the ruins of one of the most important cities of pre-Columbian America. Since the name of the city and its inhabitants had been lost to memory, they were given the name of the small nearby village.

When the Spaniards reached this place in the sixteenth century, they were introduced to the legend that Tiahuanaco had been built in the course of a single night by a race of giants in a long-ago age, far more ancient than the Incas. The legend also held that because of the many sins of its inhabitants, a god had emerged from Lake Titicaca and transformed them all into statues, in order to make way for the creation of a new humanity. Subsequent investigations have turned up countless legends concerning this city throughout the Andean world.

From the time of the Spanish conquest, the ruins of Tiahuanaco have fascinated generations of explorers, travelers, scholars, and the public at large. Few sites have been the subject of as much speculation as this one. Some have claimed that the city is twelve thousand years old; others have maintained that it was the "cradle of humanity in the Americas." Myth and reality, science and fiction have intertwined to give Tiahuanaco an enigmatic allure. The fact of the matter is that our information about the culture that produced the city is so fragmentary that for the most part we can only speculate about its true character. Still, things are slowly changing. Research at the site and in the surrounding area of influence is gradually helping us to put together various bits and pieces of the mosaic. Even though a great deal more study will be necessary before we are able to provide an accurate picture of the history of Tiahuanaco, the conclusions that we can draw now are no less captivating than the most audacious fantasies.

Archaeologists believe that Tiahuanaco was the capital of one of the largest indigenous states in the ancient Americas. The culture that developed on this site between the third and the twelfth centuries C.E. was, in fact, one of the most important factors in the complex cultural history of the Andes.

Lake Titicaca is an enormous freshwater sea set in the midst of the Andean peaks. Around the lake are plains flanked by the Cordillera Real and the Western Cordillera. Spanish chroniclers refer to this lake basin as the *Collao,* meaning the region of *los Collas,* the highlands. It is a cold, harsh region, whipped by implacable winds and subject to abrupt changes in temperature from day to night. The average altitude is about four thousand meters (13,100 ft.) above sea level, the boundary condition for the survival of animals and plants. The rainy season is brief but productive. Cycles of drought alternate unpredictably with cycles of heavy weather, producing sudden floods and freezes. At first glance, it would not seem to be a very hospitable place for humans to settle, and yet it was one of the most densely populated areas in America before the Spaniards arrived. It has been estimated that there were between one and three million people living here when the Europeans arrived.

The ancient Andeans held that the earth was worth very little unless there was someone to work it. The most important consideration for them was the amount of human energy available to be put to work. Therefore, the large human population in the Collao must have constituted a considerable incentive to the expansionistic aims of one empire after another. In any event, Tiahuanaco stood as a power for thousands of years before the Incas conquered this territory with stunning swiftness in the fifteenth century.

A culture does not spring fully formed out of nothing. It is always the product of a long and complicated process, during which local development and cultural influences originating in other regions flow together until a synthesis is attained — a synthesis that typically represents only one instant in a long process of gestation. In fact, if human settlements had not worked to adapt to the hostile physical environment in the area long before the rise of Tiahuanaco, no culture would have been able to develop on the highlands. The central threat to human survival was the exceedingly great elevation, which contributed to a variety of chronic and potentially catastrophic maladies. On the other hand, the adverse natural conditions of the Collao also seem to have fired the imagination and ingenuity of the highlands communities in powerful ways, inducing them to find solutions to the wide-ranging problems. In time, they domesticated the hardy indigenous flora (various grasses and tubers) and fauna (the llama and the alpaca). They exploited the extreme temperatures to dry and conserve foodstuffs such as meat and potatoes. And they perfected methods for the construction of durable dwellings and the extraction and casting of metals — technological processes of incalculable social and economic importance. Equally important was the assembly of a communications network covering a vast region of the south-central Andes, which encouraged the formation of an increasingly complex and populous society on the shores of Lake Titicaca.

About one thousand years before Tiahuanaco acquired its fame, a great series of cultures flourished on the highlands that can now be recognized chiefly through their typology of ceramics: the Qualuyu, the Cusipata, the Chiripa, and — later — the Kalasasaya and the Pukara cultures. Around 500 B.C.E., contacts among the various villages began to become increasingly intense, as evidenced by increasing similarities in ceramic artifacts from the sites. Later on, contacts intensified with the Paracas culture along the southern coast of Peru, the Chanapata culture in Cuzco, and the Wankarani culture in the northern and northeastern areas around Lake Poopó. The era of the Pukara, a culture with Andean and Amazonian roots, dominated the cultural landscape for the next six centuries.

In the course of this period, the settlements that developed near the lake continued to be "village" settlements, but scattered small groups survived as well. At the same time, further south in the context of the Chiripa culture, the first traces of temple architecture began to appear.

Important changes began to take place at the end of this period, when the Pukara became a complex society. In the place that bears this name, situated some eighty kilometers (50 mi.) northwest of Lake Titicaca, the people built a pyramid and a number of temples, one of which was semi-subterranean. Stone sculptures of great quality and exceedingly refined ceramics with engraved patterns and figures painted in various colors also made their appearance. One of the most interesting designs is that of a personage holding a scepter in one hand and a cord tied around the neck of a llama in the other hand; its position makes this figure reminiscent of the "Personage of the Scepters" of Chavín. Among the various designs are those of personages portrayed with axes, trophy-heads, decapitated bodies, and the like; these figures are inevitably depicted in profile, as if straining to look upward. This latter iconographic typology is recurrent in Pukara art, and is also found in the stone sculptures, which would seem to suggest that special attention might have been devoted to victims of human sacrifice.

There is a striking resemblance between the depictions of the ancient natives of Pukara in ritual positions and the appearance of modern-day Amazonian Indios taking part in the ritual consumption of hallucinogens and associated rites. Undoubtedly, the Pukara artifacts are depictions of shamanistic figures — witch doctors, profound experts on herbs, presumed to have remarkable powers, including the capacity to mediate between human communities and the world of spirits. The fact that many of these depictions have been found in areas quite distant from Pukara, such as the south-central and central Andes, suggests that there might have been wandering shamans who sought to spread knowledge of their practices and their beliefs. The monumental structure of the ceremonial center of Pukara speaks eloquently of the power of the chiefs and of their ability to assemble large workforces, probably with the help of these wandering shamans.

Pukara became an important stopping point for

llama caravans, which gave increasing prestige to the organizers of these exchanges. Moreover, the nearby *punas* — the high, cold, arid plateaus of the Peruvian Andes — were perfectly suited for raising alpacas and llamas, while the surrounding plains constituted an excellent terrain in which to cultivate tubers.

Apparently, the first *qochas* (large circular, oblong, or rectangular depressions dug in the earth), which can still be seen in the area, were a product of Pukara society. Running as deep as six meters (20 ft.), they were used to gather and store rainfall for use in farming. Rainwater would remain in the *qochas* for long periods of time and could sustain agriculture during the driest seasons of the year. The water level was controlled through a complex system of canals that linked neighboring depressions, enabling farmers to irrigate the planted fields within the depressions, which also served to shelter the crops from winds and from freezing. The *qochas* were also used to store water and fodder for herds of llamas and alpacas.

Design on Pukara ceramics: two figures with scepter and symbolic elements. These could well be "roaming shamans."

Following pages: Totora vessels called balsa de totora, *still used by Uru Indios, on the Peruvian banks of Lake Titicaca.*

A group of alpacas grazing at 3,000 meters (9,840 ft.) above sea level on the highlands of the Western Cordillera.
(Photograph by Mireille Vautier)

3 The Earliest Phases of Tiahuanaco

WHEN THE SITE of Pukara had already become a prestigious religious ceremonial center, the place where Tiahuanaco was later to rise was still occupied by Kalasasaya, one of the many village societies of the region, struggling to improve its way of life. Kalasasaya stood in a location that was strategic for caravan traffic and apparently maintained close links with Pukara.

It is believed that, during the same period, the Chiripa society was making enormous efforts to develop systems of cultivation similar to those used at Pukara in order to increase its agricultural production. Unlike Pukara, the Chiripa constructed small elevated fields and developed systems of cultivation that were later further refined and used on a much larger scale in the context of the culture of Tiahuanaco. These agricultural innovations were motivated by a need to produce increasing quantities of food to support the growing population of the southern section of the Titicaca basin and to supply the demand for agricultural products among groups living outside the highlands, in areas served by caravan traffic.

The general increase in caravan traffic around the time Tiahuanaco was founded suggests that it was a period of substantial change throughout the Collao. The territories surrounding Lake Titicaca must have been the subject of great contention, particularly the more populous and productive territories. The human population in this region may well have been subjected to periodic food shortages. It appears, however, that this imbalance between population and resources — a cyclical phenomenon in the history of the region — paradoxically became one of the great forces propelling the cultural development of the Collao.

It is believed that the site of Tiahuanaco became one of the most important settlements in the Collao because of its strategic location near the southern end of the lake. The area quickly emerged as a point of convergence for the routes of the llama caravans that brought goods to and from various sites. Commercial traffic contributed to the growth in power and prestige of the village chiefs, who were elected by the community. Their job was to control the flow of economic goods that had a special im-

A four-pointed hat, woven out of multicolored llama wool. This type of hat was worn throughout the highlands during the period of Tiahuanaco's influence.

portance to the population, such as maize, chili peppers, coca, and other imported products. By redistributing these products among the various groups that formed the villages, the chiefs acquired reputations for being generous, competent, and trustworthy. At the same time, the sacrificing shamans also began to play an increasingly important role in Tiahuanacan society, much as they had at Pukara. A stone architrave found in the sector of Kantatayta amid the ruins of Tiahuanaco is engraved with four mythological figures that are strikingly similar to the images of the sacrificers that appear on Pukara ceramics. Common elements between the iconography of Pukara and the architrave of Kantatayta include the figure's holding a scepter in one hand and symbols of human sacrifice in the other, crossed canine teeth, and what seems to be a symbol for the consumption of hallucinogens emerging from its mouth.

It is believed that the interests of the shaman-priests and those of the village chiefs eventually began to coincide, and the shaman-priests started officiating at certain "rites of sanctification" that conferred a degree of validation to matters that had previously had no social sanction, such as the transmission of powerful positions of authority solely among members of certain social classes. The shamanistic ideology, therefore, became essential to the perpetuation of the power of the ruling class.

Through the role that they played as teachers or sages in the community, the shaman-priests had sole responsibility for establishing the calendar of rites and other activities associated with agriculture and the breeding and raising of livestock. They "spoke" with the mountains, springs, caves, and certainly with the sun and moon and all of the forces that were associated with the various forms of productive activity. Only they were believed to know how to combat drought, chill, torrential rains, and flooding.

With the rise of the priestly class, Tiahuanaco was on its way to becoming first a "sacred place," then the "center of the world," and finally the capital of a theocratic state featuring a magnificent monumental architecture (the city was built between 200 and 700 C.E.). In a sense, it was going through the same process that brought Chavín to its position of power a thousand years earlier.

Ceremonial urn adorned with the figure of the god of clubs of Tiahuanaco, from Pachec (Ica, Peru).

Stone idol depicting the god of clubs of Tiahuanaco. Pucar culture.

Following double-page spread:
On the bank of Lake Titicaca a traveler from the coast receives directions to a village in which a ceremonial center is being built.

4 The Great Periods of Tiahuanaco

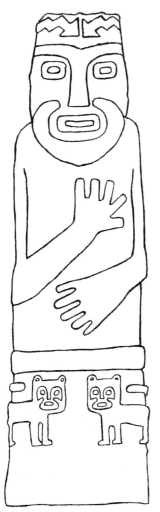

Drawing of an anthropomorphic monolith dating from the earliest phases of Tiahuanaco.

Facing page, top: *Detail of fabric with stylized anthropomorphic motifs in red, yellow, and black.*
Bottom: *Schematic plan of the central sector of the city of Tiahuanaco.*
a. *ruins of a building;*
b. *enclosure known as the Palace of Sarcophagi;*
c. *the Kalasasaya (see Chapter V);*
d. *semi-subterranean temple;*
e. Akapana, *a man-made mound, originally sheathed with blocks of stone;*
1. *entrance to the Palace of Sarcophagi;*
2. *remains of ancient tombs;*
3. *Sun Gate;*
4. *Ponce monolith;*
5. *access stairway to Kalasasaya;*
6. *the* Fraile.

THE CULTURE OF Tiahuanaco developed autonomously over a period of more than two thousand years. The line of development can be broken down into various stages, but a core of fundamental characteristics remained consistent throughout the whole period.

Around 1000 B.C.E., Tiahuanaco was nothing more than a small village, one of many others in the northern section of the highlands. It was made up of rectangular houses with pitched roofs made of clay and plant fibers and associated circular buildings that were used mostly for cooking. Through the villages ran narrow streets, some of which were paved with stone. At that time, the streets symbolized social solidarity among the various family groups.

The villagers depended on agriculture for most of their food. The chief crops were potatoes and another edible tuber called *oca*. These products were dried and stored to provide food from one annual harvest to the next.

At the outset there were no social classes at Tiahuanaco. Men and women lived in the same community structure, and labor was collective and universal. War was practically unknown. Trade supplemented the local economy. The principal import was obsidian, which was used to make arrow heads and blades. Other minerals also arrived from surrounding areas, and metallurgy was practiced. Artifacts made of copper, gold, and silver have been found at the site.

Ceramics were generally painted red on a light yellowish-chestnut background. Sometimes they were decorated with engravings and motifs outlined in red, dark gray, and white. The ceramics used on a daily basis tended to be undecorated.

No temple structures from this period have been found. The dead were buried in special trenches dug in the earth, often together with grave goods. Cinnabar was used as a colorant, and its dark red hue had a great symbolic significance. Deformation of the cranium through compression against boards was quite common, probably for aesthetic reasons. The development of Tiahuanaco was quite limited during this period, probably because the economy was largely self-sufficient, which naturally limited the need for trade and other contacts with the larger world.

During the first few centuries of the Common Era, Tiahuanaco experienced a revolution. Specifically, it evolved from a village into a city, a change that led to a series of profound consequences, the first and foremost of which was the creation of a state structure. The urban stage can be subdivided into an ancient phase, which lasted about 350 years, and a phase of maturity, which lasted about 200 years.

Evidence from aerial photography and archaeological work suggests that the ancient city of Tiahuanaco measured 2.8 kilometers (1.75 mi.) in length by 1.6 kilometers (1 mi.) in width at its greatest reaches, covering a total of 420 hectares (1,037 acres). In ancient times, the main core of the city consisted of a civic and religious center with temples and palaces; the population lived in a complex of lesser surrounding buildings. The city was laid out along two perpendicular axes, one running north-south, and the other running east-west. The step pyramid of Akapana stood at the intersection of these two axes. The rigorous astronomical orientation of the main grid toward geographic north strongly indicates that Tiahuanaco was a planned city. Most of the buildings were rectangular and were separated one from another by open spaces that also served as roadways.

The development of Tiahuanaco and its transition from the status of village to that of an urban center was made possible by a substantial overproduction of food. The peasants who worked the land would have been able to survive on one-third of the food they actually produced. The surplus was used to maintain a dominant aristocracy and to pay for new building. This surplus economy produced considerable social differentiation. At the top was an aristocracy made up of rulers, an administrative bureaucracy, priests, and warriors; there was a middle class made up of craftspeople; and at the bottom were the peasants. During the mature urban phase, considerable resources were invested in efforts to perfect and embellish the city's temples and palaces. The state assumed the cost for the construction of monuments and for overseeing the work that went on in the intervals between one type of agricultural activity and another.

Four other cities lay at the geographic heart of the Tiahuanaco culture: Wancani (28 km./18 mi. to the south of Tiahuanaco), Lukurmata and Pajchiri (12 km./8 mi. and 23 km./14 mi. to the north, respectively), and Ojje, on the Copacabana peninsula in Lake Titicaca. Beyond these urban areas lay a number of increasingly rural satellite village communities.

A movement toward cultural expansion began during the mature urban phase that broadly benefited farmers and metalworkers. During the ancient phase, Tiahuanaco grew mostly by subjugating surrounding peoples, but during the later phase, it grew by colonizing previously unoccupied territories, in the process expanding its need for maize, wood, and other valued products. Agricultural production expanded to the point that even the peasants were able to accumulate enough surplus to establish a rural barter economy. The general increase in population, wealth, and occupied land laid the foundations for Tiahuanaco's subsequent imperial stage.

Among the artifacts recovered from this period are evidences of some relatively advanced metallurgy. Copper, gold, and silver were used mostly for the production of luxury goods. Battle axes and specialized hooks used to hold large blocks of stone together have also been uncovered.

The ceramics of this period attained a remarkable level. The artistic ceramics were polychrome and had a number of variant forms, some of them embellished with decorations in relief. The kitchen utensils and tableware used in the countryside were less refined than those used in the city. Cooking implements, jars used for the storage of *chicha* (beer made of maize, a traditional beverage in the Andean area), and water jars were present in every family residence.

Sculpture attained a remarkable degree of sophistication during the mature urban phase. The facades of buildings and stelas show patterns and motifs engraved with considerable skill, indicating the use of tools such as chisels and drills. Calendar inscriptions are also present on some figures. The working of bone objects led to a great array of tools and utensils, including some used in the production of cloth and textiles. The jeweler's art was also practiced with remarkable results, especially in the area of personal ornaments.

Religion played a fundamental role during this period. Considerable architectural and artistic resources were devoted to the construction of the buildings intended for worship. Graves were usually made of stone. Bodies were interred in a squatting position, along with an array of grave goods that were meant to accompany them on their voyage to the world beyond.

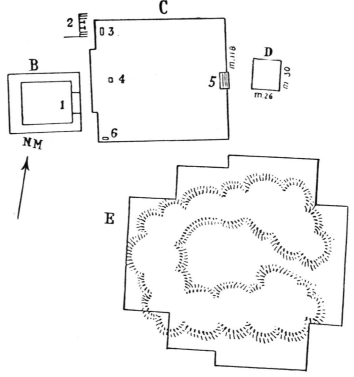

*Incense burner in the form of a feline.
Tiahuanaco culture.*
(Chilean Museum of Pre-Columbian Art,
Santiago, Chile)

Ritual goblet, or quero, *painted with
a figure representing a feline-serpent.
Tiahuanaco culture.*
(Chilean Museum of Pre-Columbian Art,
Santiago, Chile)

Facing page: *The Ponce Monolith,
situated on the interior of the
Kalasasaya of Tiahuanaco.*
(Photograph by Mireille Vautier)

5 The Great Monuments of Tiahuanaco

THE BEST-KNOWN BUILDING in Tiahuanaco is certainly the great rectangular enclosure known as Kalasasaya (from the Aymara language, in which *kala saya saya* means "many stones"). When Carlos Ponce Sanguinés began excavating the site, only a few elongated stones could be seen jutting straight up from the ground, the only visible evidence of the structure's great wall. Fully excavated, the enclosure, which is oriented in line with the four cardinal points of the compass, measures 128 meters (420 ft.) from east to west and 118 meters (327 ft.) from north to south. A broad stairway along the eastern side of the enclosure leads to a large rectangular inner courtyard. In the rear half of this courtyard, another rectangular platform was erected, and it is here that two other famous monuments are located. One is the Sun Gate, which had collapsed but was rebuilt at the beginning of this century, near the northwest corner of Kalasasaya. This is a monolithic block of andesite measuring three meters (about 10 ft.) in height by almost four meters (13 ft.) in width, and with an average thickness of sixty centimeters (2 ft.). A rectangular aperture was cut

through the center of the slab (hence the name, Sun Gate). On the upper part of the slab, looking east, is a group of figures engraved in the distinctive geometrical style of Tiahuanaco. A single human figure is carved at the center, shown face-on, with a large square head surrounded by rays, zoomorphic appendages, and an elaborate pectoral; this figure is shown holding two scepters terminating in two condor heads. On either side of this figure — certainly a deity, and possibly the god Viracocha — are four rows of figures, two of which are made up of winged men. The third row contains men with the heads of condors standing in profile, looking toward the central figure. The fourth row, which is the lowest, presents several smaller versions of the central figure, all facing forward. The entire array has been variously interpreted by such scholars as Max Uhle, Posnansky, Tello, Pucher, and others, and more recently by Buck, Ibarra Grasso, and Vivante. The task of interpreting all these elements is indeed daunting and remains controversial, but there is at least agreement on the point that the Sun Gate is rich in profound religious symbolism.

Near the southwest corner of Kalasasaya stands the earliest known anthropomorphic monolith, traditionally called "The Monk" because of its hieratic pose. Another slightly larger monolith in the same style was discovered around 1960 near the central area, during the excavations carried out by Ponce Sanguinés, and was named Ponce. The personage depicted on this monolith is wearing a headdress; its arms hang alongside its body, supporting two *keros,* drum vases characteristic of Tiahuanaco. The figure's clothing is rich in decorative engravings.

To the east of Kalasasaya is a smaller rectangular enclosure that must have served as a ceremonial plaza much like the interior courtyard described above. It measures 28.5 meters (about 94 ft.) from north to south and 26 meters (about 85 ft.) from east to west; the floor lies 1.7 meters (almost 6 ft.) below natural ground level. The side walls are formed from vertical pylons alternating with small stone blocks and contain several tenoned carved heads reminiscent of the Chavín typology. A stairway located on the south side provided access to the temple. Several stelae were found in the interior of the enclosure with characteristics similar to those of the "Monk" and the "Ponce."

To the south of these constructions is a mound about 200 meters (656 ft.) on each side called the Akapana. It is approximately 15 meters (50 ft.) tall, and there is evidence of a well shaft in its upper section, suggesting that it was probably part of a cistern for water.

Another rectangular enclosure has been uncovered to the west of Kalasasaya. Its outer wall measures 60 × 66 meters (197 × 217 ft.). An inner

The so-called Sun Gate in Tiahuanaco. This symbolic portal, 2.75 meters (108 in.) in height, has always been one of the most famous and variously interpreted monuments found in the Andean region.

enclosure measuring 40 × 48 meters (131 × 158 ft.) was called *Putuni* ("Palace of the Sarcophagi") because several stone containers similar to sarcophagi were found within it. Further west is another palace, called *Kheri-Kala;* all that remains of it are a series of badly damaged walls measuring 40 × 30 meters (131 × 99 ft.). Still further to the west is the "Pantheon" (a name given by Posnansky), the entrance of which was constituted by a monolithic slab smaller than the Sun Gate, called the Moon Gate. About 1.5 kilometers south of Akapana is another section of the ancient city, at the center of which is a pyramidal construction called *Puma-Punku,* meaning "the gate of the puma."

Digs carried out between 1988 and 1990 at the northwestern base of Akapana uncovered more than twenty human skeletons, almost all of them incomplete, belonging to individuals of varying ages, accompanied by offerings of animals and polychrome ceramics, some of which were intentionally broken. This discovery has been dated to about the Fourth, or Classic period (around 400-750 C.E.) and is considered to be evidence of a ritual offering to the building, the holiest in the city, and, through the building, to the god Viracocha, believed to be the creator of the world. This is the earliest evidence we have of mass human sacrifices within the kingdom of Tiahuanaco. The name given to the ruins (*Taypicala,* "the stone in the middle"), suggests that this place was considered to be the center of the world. The Akapana, symbol of the sacred mountain and the *axis mundi,* doubtless received the choicest sacrifices — children and men chosen as "food" for the divine hierarchy. This constituted the ideological foundation of Toltec and Aztec sacrifices as well.

The Moon Gate, entrance to the so-called pantheon. The frieze on the upper section is similar to the lower strip found in the Sun Gate.

Drawing of a detail of the upper part of the Sun Gate: the central deity (Viracocha?) is shown holding two scepters terminating in condor heads.

185

Sector of restored ruins at Tiahuanaco, the ancient Andean metropolis that is situated 3,840 meters (11,705 ft.) above sea level. On the right is the small semi-subterranean temple. On the left is the east side of the large rectangular enclosure known as Kalasasaya.
(Photograph by the author)

Right: *Detail of the outside covering wall of the small semi-subterranean temple in which there are a number of tenoned carved heads.*
(Photograph by Mireille Vautier)

6 The Great Periods of Tiahuanaco: The Imperial Stage

Facing page: *Wood and stone wooden squares designed to hold a hallucinogenic powder that was prepared from various plant substances. They were found in tombs in the area around Atacama. The decorations show the influence of Tiahuanaco.*

Below: *Lines of the cultural expansion of Tiahuanaco in Peru. Between 900 and 1200* C.E., *the city of Huari became the capital of an empire that extended from the Sierra to the north coast.*

THE THIRD PHASE in the development of Tiahuanaco has been described as the "imperial stage." The previous period had brought moderate expansion, but the imperial stage brought expansion on a vast scale, mostly as a result of military action. This dramatic growth had different effects in different parts of the emerging empire. Regions of established high culture (such as those on the coast and in the central Sierra of Peru) tended to develop a synthesis between the old and the new cultures; regions with a lower preexisting cultural level (including certain zones of the Andean area) tended to undergo a process of transculturation.

In the end, the empire came to include the Pacific coast, the Sierra and the highlands, and the mesothermal valleys to the east and southeast — an overall area of about 600,000 square kilometers (231,600 sq. mi.) with a considerable wealth of special resources and agricultural potential. At its height during the eleventh century, the empire is estimated to have had a population of 3.6 million, with a population density of roughly 6 inhabitants per square kilometer (16 per sq. mi.). During this period, the capital city of Tiahuanao is believed to have been inhabited by 100,000 individuals (238 people per hectare, or 96 per acre). The only European city of this era to have supported a comparably large population was Paris. Evidence from surviving place names suggests that the inhabitants of Tiahuanaco spoke a language now called Aymara.

We can probably best understand this period of expansion, which resulted in a culture that archaeologists now call the "pan-Andean horizon," by looking at it in a political context, although there are significant religious components as well. Despite the vast geographical reach of the empire, no viceroys were ever employed to oversee the administration of the outlying regions. The ruling power appears to have been largely military. The discovery of bronze and associated technological developments helped to produce an overwhelming military superiority. Indeed, the possession of metallurgically advanced weapons was a powerful incentive to expansion, which began around 700 C.E. and gave rise to a form of imperial state administration that served as the foundation of the subsequent Incan empire. The colonial foundations established during the earlier stage were clearly key to later development of the empire, inasmuch as the colonized areas became important centers in the new imperial dominion.

Wars became quite frequent. The empire supported a "professional" army and a sort of warrior class, which included "puma warriors" and "eagle warriors" (found also in Mesoamerica), groups with distinctive features that were tied to the religious system. Many stone sculptures, ceramic decorations, and fabric designs give us indications of the appearance of these warriors, with their distinctive zoomorphic masks, metal combat axes, and head-trophies taken from vanquished enemies.

For reasons that remain unclear, the empire collapsed and Tiahuanaco lost its position of power sometime around the twelfth century. There is no evidence of a natural cataclysm or invasions by outsiders, and so we can only speculate that there must have been some sort of political breakdown, perhaps associated with a period of poor harvests and food shortages. In any event, the inhabitants of the highlands subsequently arrayed

ECUADOR

COLOMBIA

BRAZIL

PACHACAMAC/Huari

HUARI • CONCHAPATA

PACHECO

PACIFIC OCEAN

TIAHUANACO

CHILE

themselves in local lordships, all speaking the Aymara tongue. Among them were Colla, on the northeast shores of Lake Titicaca; Lupaka to the west; Umasuyo to the east; Pakasa, Karanka, and Lipi to the south; and Charka at Cochabamba, Karakara to the north of Potosí, and Chicha further south. Several scholars have characterized these new regional groups as "kingdoms," but this term seems inexact, because they supported no hereditary monarchs as such. The evidence suggests that populations tended to engage in futile civil wars and otherwise decline into barbarism.

It has become commonplace to think that the Colla, who established their capital near the northwestern shore of Lake Titicaca, were the last survivors of the dismantling of the empire of Tiahuanaco, although the archaeological evidence for this supposition is quite thin. At most it seems to point to them as the leading link between Tiahuanaco and the Incas. When Spanish invaders asked about the origins of Andean civilization three centuries later, the inhabitants of Cuzco said that the earliest representative had come from Collao. The god Viracocha first emerged from the waters of Titicaca, they said; he created the sun and moon, turned an earlier race of people into stone, and at Tiahuanaco created human beings as the Andeans knew them. He gave names and customs to each nation and tribe and ordered them to occupy all the earth. The legend further states that among the people scattered to distant places by the god's command were the earliest Incas, who went on to found the kingdom and empire that bore their name.

This tale both emphasizes the holiness of Lake Titicaca and attests to the prestige that the culture of Tiahuanaco continued to enjoy in the Andean region many years after its decline. The Incan sovereigns asserted that they were descendants of the inhabitants of Tiahuanaco as a means of establishing their right to form an empire of their own.

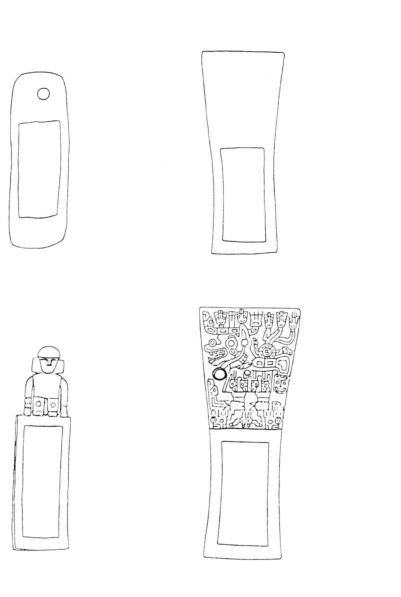

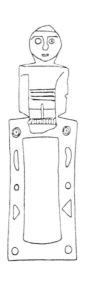

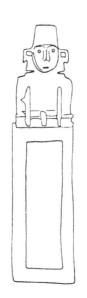

Two views of Sillustani, of the Colla culture. The ancient ruins stand on a small peninsula on the banks of the Laguna of Umayo.
(Photograph by Mireille Vautier)

7 The Late Period

THERE IS AN interesting parallel between the two principal core cultural areas in the Americas. The Late Andean phase is similar in a number of ways the Mesoamerican Postclassic period. Like the Toltecs in Mexico, the Huari culture — which developed in the seventh century in the valley of Ayacucho — played a very important role within the Andean region. A century or two after this culture's birth, it began to expand toward the southern and central areas of Peru, incorporating the older region of Moche on the northern coast.

Huari was a fully planned city, and it served as a model for other urban centers that survived the collapse of this empire, a forerunner to the Incas. At the outset, Huari was greatly influenced by the cul-

Chased sheet-silver pectoral with pendents. Chimú culture.
(Museo del Banco Central de Reserve del Perù, Lima)

ture of Nazca, and later by that of Tiahuanaco, from which it borrowed both artistic styles and religious symbolism. It went into decline in the twelfth century, however, the victim of a sharp shift in the climate and civil rebellion, reverting to a collection of local kingdoms reminiscent of the Classic period. The best known sites are those of Chimor and Chimú on the northern coast, Chancay and Chinca along the central and southern coast, and Colla, Lupaka, and other lesser sites in the highlands.

The kingdom of Chimú occupied the valleys of the arid northern coast of Peru and a few areas verging on the Sierra. The economy was based on agriculture and trade in crafted objects. The main settlement of the Chimú was Chan-Chan, an enormous urban complex made up of a series of rectangular walled quarters or sectors, each with its own temple or palace, storehouses, cisterns, and similar structures. The adobe walls are adorned by handsome geometric and zoomorphic bas-reliefs in a style that took its inspiration from fabric design. Chimú ceramics continued to employ the ancient tradition of stirrup handles; it was not polychrome, but rather black or dark grey, and had a typically metallic sheen obtained through a special combination of oxidation and polishing. The objects were produced with molds and mostly featured depictions that were naturalistic in style, with images of fruit, animals, and small human figures predominating. The Chimú were also specialists in working precious metal; they made utensils, ornaments, and solid, concave, and laminated figures from silver and gold. The Chimú set up a small empire, defended to the south by the fortress of Paramonga and by a great wall that stretched all the way to the foot of the Andes. This empire was overrun by the Incas in the second half of the sixteenth century.

The origins of the state and the dynasty of the Incas remain shrouded in mystery and legend. Their history began with a local kingdom that broke away from the Huari empire. The succession to the throne in 1438 of the Inca Yupanqui (a great statesman dubbed *Pachacuti,* meaning "He who begins a new era") marked the beginning of the expansion and organization of the Tahuantinsuyu, or empire of "the four regions," corresponding roughly to the four points of the compass. The capital city was Cuzco ("umbilicus of the world"), one of the greatest pre-Columbian cities in the Americas, situated in a high valley, some 3,400 meters (11,150 ft.) above sea level. The Incas spread out from this city into the Andean valleys and highlands, eventually reaching the Pacific coast (in a later phase), though always shunning the eastern forests. Archaeological data has confirmed some of the details of the oral tradition still alive at the time of the Spanish conquest, which tells of three successive sovereigns who conquered and organized the

Ollantaytambo. In the distance is the building known as the Hall of Ten Niches. On the right is the gate that leads to the top of the fortifications that overlook the residential section.
(Photograph by Mireille Vautier)

Empire. The first of these was Pachacuti Inca Yupanqui (ruled 1438-1463), whose principal conquests were areas of Peru around Cuzco and the Colla kingdom on Lake Titicaca. Between 1463 and 1471, he and his son Tupac Inca Yupanqui conquered the Chimú kingdom and a number of areas in the Ecuadorian Sierra. After Pachacuti Inca Yupanqui, Tupac Inca Yupanqui (ruled 1471-1493) conquered the south-central coast of Peru, the southern portion of the Bolivian highland, the northeast of Argentina, and the northern and central areas of Chile. The third sovereign, Huayna Capac (ruled 1493-1525), expanded and consolidated the Inca possessions in Ecuador, where he founded a secondary capital, Quito.

The elder son and legitimate successor to Huayna Capac was Huascar. He proved incapable of holding the empire together, however, and his stepbrother Atahuallpa took advantage of his weakness to launch a brutal and bloody civil war. The Spaniards, led by Francisco Pizarro, capitalized on the internecine strife to press their own advantage. They took Atahuallpa prisoner in 1532 and held him until his death the following year. The founding of Lima on the central coast marked the end of the Inca's social and political domination, although the ancient tradition survived among the natives of the Sierra and the highlands for some time.

The Incas were the heirs to more than three millennia of Andean cultural and technological development. Their originality manifested itself chiefly in the administrative organization of their empire (one of history's greatest empires) and in the intensely hierarchical system that was centralized around the sovereign Inca, who was held to be the Son of the Sun (the chief deity of the state). The Incas constructed an elaborate network of roads linking all their territories; they were used by the famous *chasquis* (imperial messengers, or runners), who transported urgent messages or goods. Religious rites were performed atop the highest peaks to propitiate the gods of the heavens or of fertility. The Incas were masters of monumental architecture who managed to fit huge blocks of stone together with great precision. The fortresses of Sacsayhuaman near Cuzco and the cities of Machu Picchu and Ollantaytambo are the best known examples of their skillful work, but there are many such architectural triumphs. In addition to their cities, they terraced and specially treated slopes for cultivation, dug irrigation canals, strung bridges over the mightiest streams, sunk mines, and produced workshops for the working of metals.

On the whole, their ceramics represent a far lower level of quality, perhaps because they were produced on an almost industrial scale. One of the few objects in this category that exhibits a certain degree of originality is the *aribalo,* a ceramic vase with a narrow neck and a slightly conical base, typically decorated with white, black, and red geometric patterns and designs. Generally speaking, the crafts of the Incas give evidence of a synthesis of ancient beliefs, religious practices, and the imperial cult.

Oddly, the inhabitants of this great empire had no formal system of writing; records were kept with help of the mnemonic system of the *quipu,* multicolored knotted strings that were interpreted by *quipu-camayoc.*

Following pages: *A platform of unfired clay with bas-reliefs of mythical figures and probably a rainbow at Huaca El Dragón, not far from Trujillo. Chimú culture.*

Inca culture: Machu Picchu, sector of the Prisons. Note the high eaves of the houses supporting the large double-pitched roofs.

(Photograph by Mireille Vautier)